RECIPES FOR STRENGTH

A High-Protein Cookbook for Fitness Enthusiasts

Phil Hearth

By reading this document, the reader agrees that under no circumstances is the author responsible for any losses, direct or indirect, which are incurred as a result of the use of the information contained within this document, including, but not limited to, — errors, omissions, or inaccuracies.

Table of Contents

INTRODUCTION

Welcome to the Protein Recipe Collection! In this cookbook, we have curated a selection of delicious and nutritious recipes that are rich in protein. Protein is an essential macronutrient that plays a vital role in our overall health and well-being. Whether you are an athlete, fitness enthusiast, or simply looking to incorporate more protein into your diet, this collection is designed to inspire and satisfy your protein needs.

Why is it important to consume protein-rich foods? The benefits of a protein-rich diet are numerous. Here are some key advantages:

1. Muscle Building and Repair: Protein is the building block of muscles. Consuming an adequate amount of protein supports muscle growth, repair, and maintenance. It provides the necessary amino acids that are crucial for building and preserving lean muscle mass.
2. Satiety and Weight Management: Protein is known to be more satiating than carbohydrates or fats. Including protein in your meals can help you feel fuller for longer, reducing the chances of overeating and aiding in weight management.
3. Metabolism and Energy Production: Protein plays a role in the thermic effect of food, which means that it requires more energy to digest and metabolize compared to other macronutrients. This can slightly boost your metabolism and contribute to increased calorie burning.
4. Nutrient Absorption: Protein is involved in the transport and absorption of important nutrients, such as vitamins and minerals, in our bodies. A protein-rich diet can enhance nutrient uptake and utilization.
5. Blood Sugar Regulation: Protein can help regulate blood sugar levels by slowing down the absorption of carbohydrates, preventing sharp spikes and crashes in

blood glucose levels. This is especially beneficial for individuals with diabetes or those aiming to maintain stable energy levels throughout the day.

6. Bone Health: Protein is not only essential for muscle health but also plays a role in maintaining strong and healthy bones. It aids in calcium absorption and promotes bone density, reducing the risk of osteoporosis.

By incorporating protein-rich foods into your diet, you can enjoy these benefits and support your overall health and fitness goals. From savory dishes to delectable desserts, our protein recipes are designed to make your meals nutritious, satisfying, and enjoyable.

Remember, it's important to consult with a healthcare professional or registered dietitian to determine your specific protein needs based on your age, sex, activity level, and health conditions. Enjoy exploring the wonderful world of protein-packed recipes and nourish your body with the goodness it deserves!

BREAKFAST

Greek Yogurt with Granola and Berries

Ingredients:

- 1 cup plain Greek yogurt
- 1/2 cup mixed berries (blueberries, raspberries, strawberries)
- 1/4 cup granola
- 1 tbsp honey

Directions:

1. Add Greek yogurt to a bowl.
2. Top with mixed berries and granola.
3. Drizzle with honey and enjoy.

Nutritional Values (approximate):

- Calories: 350
- Protein: 23g
- Carbs: 45g
- Fat: 7g

Protein-Packed Avocado Toast

Ingredients:

- 2 slices whole-grain bread
- 1 ripe avocado
- 1/4 cup hummus
- 1/2 cup cooked egg whites
- Salt and pepper to taste

- Optional: red pepper flakes, fresh herbs

Directions:

1. Toast bread to your liking.
2. Mash avocado in a bowl, and spread on toasted bread.
3. Spread hummus over the avocado layer.
4. Top with cooked egg whites and season with salt and pepper.
5. Optional: sprinkle with red pepper flakes and fresh herbs.

Nutritional Values (approximate):

- Calories: 480
- Protein: 24g
- Carbs: 50g
- Fat: 23g

Overnight Protein Oats

Ingredients:

- 1/2 cup rolled oats
- 1 cup unsweetened almond milk
- 1 scoop protein powder (vanilla or chocolate)
- 1 tbsp chia seeds
- 1/2 tsp vanilla extract
- 1/2 cup diced fruit (banana, berries, or your favorite fruit)

Directions:

1. In a mason jar or container, combine oats, almond milk, protein powder, chia seeds, and vanilla extract. Mix well.
2. Cover and refrigerate overnight or at least 4 hours.

3. Remove from fridge, stir, and top with diced fruit before serving.

Nutritional Values (approximate):

- Calories: 400
- Protein: 30g
- Carbs: 45g
- Fat: 12g

Spinach and Feta Egg Muffins

Ingredients:

- 6 large eggs
- 1/2 cup chopped fresh spinach
- 1/4 cup crumbled feta cheese
- 1/4 cup diced red bell pepper
- Salt and pepper to taste

Directions:

1. Preheat oven to 350°F (180°C) and grease a 6-cup muffin tin.
2. In a large bowl, whisk eggs and add spinach, feta, and red bell pepper. Season with salt and pepper.
3. Divide mixture evenly among the muffin cups.
4. Bake for 20-25 minutes, or until eggs are set and edges are golden brown.

Nutritional Values (approximate):

- Calories: 90
- Protein: 7g

- Carbs: 2g
- Fat: 6g per muffin

Quinoa Breakfast Bowl

Ingredients:

- 1/2 cup cooked quinoa
- 1/2 cup plain Greek yogurt
- 1/4 cup mixed berries
- 1 tbsp honey
- 1 tbsp almond butter
- 1 tbsp chopped nuts (almonds, walnuts, or pecans)

Directions:

1. In a bowl, combine cooked quinoa and Greek yogurt.
2. Top with mixed berries, a drizzle of honey, almond butter, and chopped nuts.

Nutritional Values (approximate):

- Calories: 400
- Protein: 20g
- Carbs: 50g
- Fat: 16g

Veggie and Egg Breakfast Burrito

Ingredients:

- 1 large whole-grain tortilla

- 2 large eggs, scrambled
- 1/4 cup black beans, rinsed and drained
- 1/4 cup diced bell peppers
- 1/4 cup diced onions
- 1/4 cup shredded cheese
- Salt and pepper to taste
- Optional: salsa, avocado

Directions:

1. In a pan, cook scrambled eggs, bell peppers, and onions over medium heat. Season with salt and pepper.
2. Warm tortilla for 10-15 seconds in the microwave.
3. Layer the cooked egg mixture, black beans, and cheese onto the tortilla.
4. Fold the sides and roll up the tortilla, tucking in the ends as you roll.
5. Optional: serve with salsa and sliced avocado.

Nutritional Values (approximate):

- Calories: 500
- Protein: 28g
- Carbs: 58g
- Fat: 19g

Cottage Cheese and Fruit Parfait

Ingredients:

- 1 cup low-fat cottage cheese
- 1/2 cup diced fruit (pineapple, peaches, or mixed berries)
- 1/4 cup granola
- 1 tbsp honey

Directions:

1. In a glass or bowl, layer half of the cottage cheese, followed by half of the fruit and granola.
2. Repeat the layers with the remaining ingredients.
3. Drizzle honey over the top and serve.

Nutritional Values (approximate):

- Calories: 350
- Protein: 28g
- Carbs: 45g
- Fat: 8g

Protein Pancakes

Ingredients:

- 1 cup rolled oats
- 1 ripe banana
- 2 large eggs
- 1/2 cup cottage cheese
- 1/4 cup unsweetened almond milk
- 1 tsp vanilla extract
- 1/2 tsp baking powder
- Pinch of salt

Directions:

1. In a blender, combine all ingredients and blend until smooth.
2. Preheat a non-stick skillet over medium heat.
3. Pour 1/4 cup batter onto the skillet for each pancake.
4. Cook until bubbles form on the surface, then flip and cook until golden brown.

Nutritional Values (approximate):

- Calories: 350
- Protein: 20g
- Carbs: 50g
- Fat: 9g for 3 pancakes

Smoked Salmon and Cream Cheese Bagel

Ingredients:

- 1 whole-grain bagel, sliced in half
- 2 oz smoked salmon
- 2 tbsp light cream cheese
- 1 tbsp capers
- 1/4 cup sliced cucumber
- 1/4 cup thinly sliced red onion
- Fresh dill for garnish

Directions:

1. Toast the bagel halves to your liking.
2. Spread cream cheese on each half of the bagel.
3. Layer smoked salmon, cucumber slices, and red onion on top.
4. Sprinkle capers and fresh dill over the toppings.

Nutritional Values (approximate):

- Calories: 400
- Protein: 25g
- Carbs: 50g
- Fat: 12g

Power-Packed Green Smoothie

Ingredients:

- 1 cup unsweetened almond milk
- 1 cup baby spinach
- 1 ripe banana, frozen
- 1 scoop protein powder (vanilla or unflavored)
- 1 tbsp almond butter
- 1/2 cup ice

Directions:

1. Add all ingredients to a blender.
2. Blend on high until smooth and creamy.

Nutritional Values (approximate):

- Calories: 350
- Protein: 25g
- Carbs: 40g
- Fat: 12g

Turkey, Egg, and Cheese Breakfast Sandwich

Ingredients:

- 1 whole-grain English muffin, sliced in half
- 2 slices turkey bacon
- 1 large egg, cooked to your preference
- 1 slice low-fat cheese

Directions:

1. Toast the English muffin halves to your liking.
2. Cook the turkey bacon in a pan over medium heat until crispy.
3. Assemble the sandwich by layering the turkey bacon, egg, and cheese on one half of the muffin.
4. Top with the other half of the muffin and enjoy.

Nutritional Values (approximate):

- Calories: 350
- Protein: 25g
- Carbs: 30g
- Fat: 15g

Cheddar and Veggie Frittata

Ingredients:

- 6 large eggs
- 1/2 cup shredded cheddar cheese
- 1/4 cup diced bell pepper
- 1/4 cup diced onion
- 1/4 cup chopped broccoli
- Salt and pepper to taste

Directions:

1. Preheat oven to 350°F (180°C) and grease an 8-inch round baking dish.
2. In a large bowl, whisk eggs and season with salt and pepper.
3. Stir in cheddar cheese, bell pepper, onion, and broccoli.
4. Pour mixture into the prepared baking dish.
5. Bake for 20-25 minutes, or until eggs are set and edges are golden brown.

Nutritional Values (approximate):

- Calories: 160
- Protein: 12g
- Carbs: 5g
- Fat: 10g per serving (1/4 frittata)

Protein-Rich Chia Seed Pudding

Ingredients:

- 1/4 cup chia seeds
- 1 cup unsweetened almond milk
- 1 scoop protein powder (vanilla or chocolate)
- 1 tbsp honey or maple syrup
- 1/2 cup mixed berries or diced fruit of your choice
- 1 tbsp chopped nuts or seeds (optional)

Directions:

1. In a mason jar or container, combine chia seeds, almond milk, protein powder, and sweetener. Mix well.
2. Cover and refrigerate overnight or for at least 4 hours.
3. Remove from fridge, stir, and top with mixed berries or fruit and nuts or seeds before serving.

Nutritional Values (approximate):

- Calories: 400
- Protein: 25g
- Carbs: 45g
- Fat: 15g

High-Protein Overnight Oats

Ingredients:

- 1/2 cup rolled oats
- 1 scoop protein powder (vanilla or chocolate)
- 1 tbsp ground flaxseed
- 1 cup unsweetened almond milk
- 1/2 cup mixed berries or diced fruit of your choice
- 1 tbsp chopped nuts or seeds (optional)

Directions:

1. In a mason jar or container, combine oats, protein powder, ground flaxseed, and almond milk. Mix well.
2. Cover and refrigerate overnight or for at least 4 hours.
3. Remove from fridge, stir, and top with mixed berries or fruit and nuts or seeds before serving.

Nutritional Values (approximate):

- Calories: 450
- Protein: 30g
- Carbs: 50g
- Fat: 15g

Greek Yogurt and Berry Parfait

Ingredients:

- 1 cup plain Greek yogurt
- 1/2 cup mixed berries (fresh or frozen)
- 1/4 cup granola
- 1 tbsp honey or maple syrup

Directions:

1. In a glass or bowl, layer half of the Greek yogurt, followed by half of the berries and granola.
2. Repeat the layers with the remaining ingredients.
3. Drizzle honey or maple syrup over the top and serve.

Nutritional Values (approximate):

- Calories: 350
- Protein: 25g
- Carbs: 45g
- Fat: 8g

Protein-Packed Avocado Toast

Ingredients:

- 2 slices whole-grain bread
- 1 ripe avocado, mashed
- 2 large eggs, cooked to your preference
- Salt and pepper to taste
- Optional toppings: sliced tomato, crumbled feta cheese

Directions:

1. Toast the bread slices to your liking.
2. Spread mashed avocado evenly over each slice.
3. Top with cooked eggs and season with salt and pepper.
4. Optionally, add sliced tomato and crumbled feta cheese.

Nutritional Values (approximate):

- Calories: 400
- Protein: 20g
- Carbs: 40g
- Fat: 20g

Spinach and Feta Breakfast Quesadilla

Ingredients:

- 1 large whole-grain tortilla
- 1/4 cup crumbled feta cheese
- 1/2 cup baby spinach leaves
- 2 large eggs, scrambled
- Salt and pepper to taste

Directions:

1. Cook scrambled eggs in a pan over medium heat. Season with salt and pepper.
2. Warm the tortilla for 10-15 seconds in the microwave.
3. Lay the tortilla flat and spread feta cheese on one half of the tortilla.
4. Add cooked eggs and spinach leaves on top of the cheese.
5. Fold the other half of the tortilla over the filling.
6. Cook the quesadilla in a pan on medium heat for 2-3 minutes per side, or until the cheese is melted and the tortilla is crispy.

Nutritional Values (approximate):

- Calories: 450
- Protein: 25g
- Carbs: 40g

- Fat: 20g

Savory Protein Oatmeal

Ingredients:

- 1/2 cup rolled oats
- 1 cup water or unsweetened almond milk
- 1/4 tsp salt
- 1/4 cup grated cheese (your choice)
- 1/2 cup cooked, chopped vegetables (spinach, bell peppers, onions)
- 1 large egg, cooked to your preference
- Optional: hot sauce, salsa, or avocado

Directions:

1. Cook oats with water or almond milk and salt according to package instructions.
2. Stir in grated cheese and cooked vegetables.
3. Top with cooked egg and any optional toppings.

Nutritional Values (approximate):

- Calories: 350
- Protein: 20g
- Carbs: 35g
- Fat: 15g

Savory Spinach and Cheese Egg Muffins

Ingredients:

- 6 large eggs
- 1 cup baby spinach, chopped
- 1/2 cup grated cheese (your choice)
- Salt and pepper to taste
- Optional: diced veggies (bell peppers, onions, tomatoes)

Directions:

1. Preheat oven to 350°F (180°C) and grease a 6-cup muffin tin.
2. In a large bowl, whisk eggs and season with salt and pepper.
3. Stir in chopped spinach and grated cheese. Optionally, add diced veggies.
4. Divide the mixture evenly among the muffin cups.
5. Bake for 20-25 minutes, or until eggs are set and edges are golden brown.

Nutritional Values (approximate):

- Calories: 120
- Protein: 10g
- Carbs: 2g
- Fat: 8g per muffin

Banana and Almond Butter Smoothie

Ingredients:

- 1 ripe banana, frozen
- 1 scoop protein powder (vanilla or unflavored)
- 2 tbsp almond butter
- 1 cup unsweetened almond milk
- 1/2 cup ice

Directions:

1. Add all ingredients to a blender.
2. Blend on high until smooth and creamy.

Nutritional Values (approximate):

- Calories: 450
- Protein: 30g
- Carbs: 40g
- Fat: 20g

Cottage Cheese and Fruit Bowl

Ingredients:

- 1 cup low-fat cottage cheese
- 1/2 cup diced fruit (such as pineapple, peaches, or mixed berries)
- 1/4 cup chopped nuts (walnuts, almonds, or pecans)
- 1 tbsp honey or maple syrup

Directions:

1. In a bowl, combine cottage cheese and diced fruit.
2. Top with chopped nuts and drizzle with honey or maple syrup before serving.

Nutritional Values (approximate):

- Calories: 350
- Protein: 25g
- Carbs: 30g
- Fat: 15g

Ham and Swiss Omelette

Ingredients:

- 3 large eggs
- 2 oz sliced ham, chopped
- 1/4 cup shredded Swiss cheese
- 1/4 cup diced onion
- 1/4 cup diced bell pepper
- Salt and pepper to taste

Directions:

1. In a medium bowl, whisk eggs and season with salt and pepper.
2. Heat a nonstick skillet over medium heat and add the diced onion and bell pepper. Cook for 2-3 minutes, or until tender.
3. Pour the whisked eggs into the skillet and cook until set on the bottom.
4. Sprinkle the chopped ham and shredded Swiss cheese on one half of the omelette.

5. Fold the other half of the omelette over the fillings and cook for an additional minute, or until the cheese is melted.

Nutritional Values (approximate):

- Calories: 400
- Protein: 35g
- Carbs: 10g
- Fat: 25g

Apple Cinnamon Protein Pancakes

Ingredients:

- 1 cup oat flour
- 1 scoop protein powder (vanilla or unflavored)
- 1 tsp baking powder
- 1/2 tsp ground cinnamon
- 1/2 cup unsweetened applesauce
- 1/2 cup milk of your choice
- 2 large eggs
- 1 tsp vanilla extract

Directions:

1. In a large bowl, mix oat flour, protein powder, baking powder, and cinnamon.
2. In a separate bowl, whisk together applesauce, milk, eggs, and vanilla extract.
3. Add wet ingredients to the dry ingredients and mix until combined.
4. Heat a nonstick skillet over medium heat and pour 1/4 cup of the batter for each pancake.

5. Cook until bubbles form on the surface, then flip and cook for another 1-2 minutes, or until golden brown.

Nutritional Values (approximate):

- Calories: 300
- Protein: 20g
- Carbs: 40g
- Fat: 6g per serving (2 pancakes)

Chocolate Protein Smoothie Bowl

Ingredients:

- 1 cup unsweetened almond milk
- 1 ripe banana, frozen
- 1 scoop chocolate protein powder
- 1 tbsp unsweetened cocoa powder
- 1/2 cup ice
- Optional toppings: sliced almonds, chia seeds, coconut flakes, fresh fruit

Directions:

1. Add almond milk, banana, protein powder, cocoa powder, and ice to a blender.
2. Blend on high until smooth and creamy.
3. Pour into a bowl and add your favorite toppings.

Nutritional Values (approximate):

- Calories: 350
- Protein: 25

SHAKE

Chocolate Protein Shake

Ingredients:

- 1 scoop of chocolate protein powder
- 250 ml almond milk
- 1 ripe banana
- 1 tablespoon of peanut butter
- 1 teaspoon of cocoa powder
- Ice cubes (optional)

Directions:

1. Place all the ingredients in a blender.
2. Blend until smooth and creamy.
3. If desired, add some ice cubes and blend again for a cooler shake.
4. Pour the shake into a glass and serve immediately.

Nutritional Information:

- Calories: 350
- Protein: 25g
- Fat: 10g
- Carbohydrates: 40g

Vanilla Strawberry Protein Shake

Ingredients:

- 1 scoop of vanilla protein powder
- 250 ml vanilla soy milk
- 1 cup of fresh strawberries
- 1 tablespoon of almond butter

- 1 teaspoon of honey (optional)
- Ice cubes (optional)

Directions:

1. Place all the ingredients in a blender.
2. Blend until smooth and creamy.
3. If desired, add some ice cubes and blend again for a cooler shake.
4. Pour the shake into a glass and serve immediately.

Nutritional Information:

- Calories: 300
- Protein: 20g
- Fat: 8g
- Carbohydrates: 35g

Coffee Protein Shake

Ingredients:

- 1 scoop of coffee-flavored protein powder
- 250 ml coconut milk
- 1 ripe banana
- 1 tablespoon of peanut butter
- 1 teaspoon of instant coffee
- Ice cubes (optional)

Directions:

1. Place all the ingredients in a blender.
2. Blend until smooth and creamy.
3. If desired, add some ice cubes and blend again for a cooler shake.

4.   Pour the shake into a glass and serve immediately.

Nutritional Information:

- Calories: 380
- Protein: 22g
- Fat: 12g
- Carbohydrates: 45g

Mixed Berry Protein Shake

Ingredients:

- 1 scoop of fruit-flavored protein powder
- 250 ml orange juice
- 1 cup of mixed berries (strawberries, raspberries, blueberries)
- 1 tablespoon of almond butter
- 1 tablespoon of honey (optional)
- Ice cubes (optional)

Directions:

1.   Place all the ingredients in a blender.
2.   Blend until smooth and creamy.
3.   If desired, add some ice cubes and blend again for a cooler shake.
4.   Pour the shake into a glass and serve immediately.

Nutritional Information:

- Calories: 320
- Protein: 18g
- Fat: 10g
- Carbohydrates: 40g

Please note that the nutritional information provided is approximate and may vary based on the specific brands of ingredients used. Enjoy your protein shakes!

Peanut Butter Banana Protein Shake

Ingredients:

- 1 scoop of vanilla protein powder
- 1 ripe banana
- 1 tablespoon of peanut butter
- 250 ml almond milk
- Ice cubes (optional)

Directions:

1. In a blender, combine the protein powder, banana, peanut butter, and almond milk.
2. Blend until smooth and creamy.
3. If desired, add ice cubes and blend again for a chilled shake.
4. Pour into a glass and serve immediately.

Nutritional Information:

- Calories: 320
- Protein: 25g
- Fat: 10g
- Carbohydrates: 30g

Blueberry Spinach Protein Shake

Ingredients:

- 1 scoop of vanilla protein powder
- 1 cup of fresh spinach
- 1/2 cup of blueberries
- 250 ml unsweetened coconut water
- Ice cubes (optional)

Directions:

1. Place the protein powder, spinach, blueberries, and coconut water in a blender.
2. Blend until well combined and smooth.
3. If desired, add ice cubes and blend again for a colder shake.
4. Pour into a glass and enjoy immediately.

Nutritional Information:

- Calories: 180
- Protein: 20g
- Fat: 2g
- Carbohydrates: 25g

Oatmeal Banana Protein Shake

Ingredients:

- 1 scoop of chocolate protein powder
- 1 ripe banana
- 1/4 cup of rolled oats
- 250 ml skim milk
- 1 tablespoon of honey (optional)

- Ice cubes (optional)

Directions:

1. Add the protein powder, banana, rolled oats, milk, and honey (if using) to a blender.
2. Blend until smooth and creamy.
3. If desired, add ice cubes and blend again for a thicker texture.
4. Pour into a glass and serve immediately.

Nutritional Information:

- Calories: 380
- Protein: 30g
- Fat: 5g
- Carbohydrates: 50g

Coconut Berry Protein Shake

Ingredients:

- 1 scoop of strawberry protein powder
- 1/2 cup of mixed berries (strawberries, raspberries, blueberries)
- 250 ml coconut milk
- 1 tablespoon of almond butter
- Ice cubes (optional)

Directions:

1. Combine the protein powder, mixed berries, coconut milk, and almond butter in a blender.
2. Blend until smooth and well combined.

3. If desired, add ice cubes and blend again for a refreshing shake.
4. Pour into a glass and enjoy immediately.

Nutritional Information:

- Calories: 290
- Protein: 22g
- Fat: 15g
- Carbohydrates: 20g

Please note that the nutritional information provided is approximate and may vary depending on the specific brands of ingredients used. Enjoy your protein shakes!

Chocolate Banana Protein Shake

Ingredients:

- 1 scoop of chocolate protein powder
- 1 ripe banana
- 250 ml almond milk
- 1 tablespoon of almond butter
- Ice cubes (optional)

Directions:

1. Place all the ingredients in a blender.
2. Blend until smooth and creamy.
3. If desired, add some ice cubes and blend again for a cooler shake.
4. Pour the shake into a glass and serve immediately.

Nutritional Information:

- Calories: 320
- Protein: 25g
- Fat: 12g
- Carbohydrates: 30g

Strawberry Coconut Protein Shake

Ingredients:

- 1 scoop of strawberry protein powder
- 1 cup of fresh strawberries
- 250 ml coconut milk
- 1 tablespoon of coconut flakes
- Ice cubes (optional)

Directions:

1. Place all the ingredients in a blender.
2. Blend until smooth and creamy.
3. If desired, add some ice cubes and blend again for a cooler shake.
4. Pour the shake into a glass and serve immediately.

Nutritional Information:

- Calories: 280
- Protein: 20g
- Fat: 10g
- Carbohydrates: 25g

Vanilla Almond Protein Shake

Ingredients:

- 1 scoop of vanilla protein powder
- 250 ml unsweetened almond milk
- 1 tablespoon of almond butter
- 1 teaspoon of honey
- Dash of cinnamon
- Ice cubes (optional)

Directions:

1. Place all the ingredients in a blender.
2. Blend until smooth and creamy.
3. If desired, add some ice cubes and blend again for a cooler shake.
4. Pour the shake into a glass and serve immediately.

Nutritional Information:

- Calories: 310
- Protein: 22g
- Fat: 15g
- Carbohydrates: 20g

Green Power Protein Shake

Ingredients:

- 1 scoop of vanilla protein powder
- 1 cup of fresh spinach
- 1/2 avocado
- 250 ml unsweetened almond milk

- 1 tablespoon of chia seeds
- Ice cubes (optional)

Directions:

1. Place all the ingredients in a blender.
2. Blend until smooth and creamy.
3. If desired, add some ice cubes and blend again for a cooler shake.
4. Pour the shake into a glass and serve immediately.

Nutritional Information:

- Calories: 290
- Protein: 20g
- Fat: 15g
- Carbohydrates: 15g

Please note that the nutritional information provided is approximate and may vary based on the specific brands of ingredients used. Enjoy your protein shakes!

◆

Peanut Butter Chocolate Protein Shake

Ingredients:

- 1 scoop of chocolate protein powder
- 250 ml almond milk
- 1 tablespoon of peanut butter
- 1 frozen banana
- 1 teaspoon of cocoa powder
- Ice cubes (optional)

Directions:

1. In a blender, combine the protein powder, almond milk, peanut butter, frozen banana, and cocoa powder.
2. Blend until smooth and creamy.
3. If desired, add ice cubes and blend again for a colder shake.
4. Pour into a glass and serve immediately.

Nutritional Information:

- Calories: 350
- Protein: 25g
- Fat: 10g
- Carbohydrates: 40g

Raspberry Coconut Protein Shake

Ingredients:

- 1 scoop of vanilla protein powder
- 250 ml coconut milk
- 1/2 cup of fresh raspberries
- 1 tablespoon of shredded coconut
- 1 tablespoon of honey
- Ice cubes (optional)

Directions:

1. Place all the ingredients in a blender.
2. Blend until smooth and creamy.
3. If desired, add some ice cubes and blend again for a cooler shake.
4. Pour the shake into a glass and serve immediately.

Nutritional Information:

- Calories: 280
- Protein: 20g
- Fat: 12g
- Carbohydrates: 25g

Matcha Green Tea Protein Shake

Ingredients:

- 1 scoop of vanilla protein powder
- 250 ml unsweetened almond milk
- 1 teaspoon of matcha green tea powder
- 1/2 frozen banana
- 1 tablespoon of almond butter
- Ice cubes (optional)

Directions:

1. In a blender, combine the protein powder, almond milk, matcha powder, frozen banana, and almond butter.
2. Blend until smooth and creamy.
3. If desired, add ice cubes and blend again for a colder shake.
4. Pour into a glass and serve immediately.

Nutritional Information:

- Calories: 290
- Protein: 22g
- Fat: 10g
- Carbohydrates: 25g

Blueberry Almond Protein Shake

Ingredients:

- 1 scoop of blueberry protein powder
- 250 ml unsweetened almond milk
- 1/2 cup of fresh blueberries
- 1 tablespoon of almond butter
- 1 tablespoon of flaxseeds
- Ice cubes (optional)

Directions:

1. Place all the ingredients in a blender.
2. Blend until smooth and creamy.
3. If desired, add some ice cubes and blend again for a cooler shake.
4. Pour the shake into a glass and serve immediately.

Nutritional Information:

- Calories: 280
- Protein: 20g
- Fat: 12g
- Carbohydrates: 25g

Please note that the nutritional information provided is approximate and may vary based on the specific brands of ingredients used. Enjoy your protein shakes!

Caramel Coffee Protein Shake

Ingredients:

- 1 scoop of caramel-flavored protein powder
- 250 ml brewed coffee, cooled
- 1 tablespoon of almond butter
- 1 teaspoon of honey
- 1/2 teaspoon of cinnamon
- Ice cubes (optional)

Directions:

1. In a blender, combine the protein powder, brewed coffee, almond butter, honey, and cinnamon.
2. Blend until smooth and well combined.
3. If desired, add ice cubes and blend again for a cooler shake.
4. Pour into a glass and serve immediately.

Nutritional Information:

- Calories: 180
- Protein: 20g
- Fat: 8g
- Carbohydrates: 10g

Mango Coconut Protein Shake

Ingredients:

- 1 scoop of vanilla protein powder
- 250 ml coconut water
- 1/2 cup of frozen mango chunks
- 1 tablespoon of shredded coconut
- 1 tablespoon of Greek yogurt
- Ice cubes (optional)

Directions:

1. Place all the ingredients in a blender.
2. Blend until smooth and creamy.
3. If desired, add some ice cubes and blend again for a cooler shake.
4. Pour the shake into a glass and serve immediately.

Nutritional Information:

- Calories: 220
- Protein: 20g
- Fat: 6g
- Carbohydrates: 25g

Chocolate Peanut Butter Banana Shake

Ingredients:

- 1 scoop of chocolate protein powder
- 1 ripe banana
- 250 ml skim milk
- 1 tablespoon of peanut butter
- 1 tablespoon of cocoa powder
- Ice cubes (optional)

Directions:

1. In a blender, combine the protein powder, banana, skim milk, peanut butter, and cocoa powder.
2. Blend until smooth and creamy.
3. If desired, add ice cubes and blend again for a colder shake.
4. Pour into a glass and serve immediately.

Nutritional Information:

- Calories: 320
- Protein: 25g
- Fat: 10g
- Carbohydrates: 35g

Raspberry Vanilla Protein Shake

Ingredients:

- 1 scoop of vanilla protein powder
- 250 ml almond milk
- 1/2 cup of fresh raspberries
- 1 tablespoon of Greek yogurt
- 1 tablespoon of honey
- Ice cubes (optional)

Directions:

1. Place all the ingredients in a blender.
2. Blend until smooth and creamy.
3. If desired, add some ice cubes and blend again for a cooler shake.
4. Pour the shake into a glass and serve immediately.

Nutritional Information:

- Calories: 200
- Protein: 20g
- Fat: 5g
- Carbohydrates: 20g

Please note that the nutritional information provided is approximate and may vary based on the specific brands of ingredients used. Enjoy your protein shakes!

Green Apple Spinach Protein Shake

Ingredients:

- 1 scoop of vanilla protein powder
- 250 ml unsweetened almond milk
- 1 green apple, cored and chopped
- Handful of fresh spinach leaves
- 1 tablespoon of almond butter
- Ice cubes (optional)

Directions:

1. Place all the ingredients in a blender.
2. Blend until smooth and creamy.
3. If desired, add some ice cubes and blend again for a cooler shake.
4. Pour the shake into a glass and serve immediately.

Nutritional Information:

- Calories: 220
- Protein: 20g
- Fat: 10g
- Carbohydrates: 20g

Coconut Pineapple Protein Shake

Ingredients:

- 1 scoop of coconut-flavored protein powder
- 250 ml coconut milk
- 1/2 cup of frozen pineapple chunks
- 1 tablespoon of shredded coconut

- 1 tablespoon of Greek yogurt
- Ice cubes (optional)

Directions:

1. Place all the ingredients in a blender.
2. Blend until smooth and creamy.
3. If desired, add some ice cubes and blend again for a cooler shake.
4. Pour the shake into a glass and serve immediately.

Nutritional Information:

- Calories: 250
- Protein: 22g
- Fat: 8g
- Carbohydrates: 25g

Chocolate Mint Protein Shake

Ingredients:

- 1 scoop of chocolate protein powder
- 250 ml unsweetened almond milk
- 1/4 teaspoon of peppermint extract
- 1 tablespoon of cacao nibs
- Ice cubes (optional)

Directions:

1. In a blender, combine the protein powder, almond milk, peppermint extract, and cacao nibs.
2. Blend until smooth and well combined.
3. If desired, add ice cubes and blend again for a cooler shake.

4. Pour into a glass and serve immediately.

Nutritional Information:

- Calories: 280
- Protein: 25g
- Fat: 10g
- Carbohydrates: 25g

Berry Blast Protein Shake

Ingredients:

- 1 scoop of mixed berry protein powder
- 250 ml unsweetened almond milk
- 1/2 cup of mixed berries (strawberries, blueberries, raspberries)
- 1 tablespoon of almond butter
- Ice cubes (optional)

Directions:

1. Place all the ingredients in a blender.
2. Blend until smooth and creamy.
3. If desired, add some ice cubes and blend again for a cooler shake.
4. Pour the shake into a glass and serve immediately.

Nutritional Information:

- Calories: 230
- Protein: 20g
- Fat: 8g
- Carbohydrates: 25g

Please note that the nutritional information provided is approximate and may vary based on the specific brands of ingredients used. Enjoy your protein shakes!

SIDES

Quinoa and Black Bean Salad

Ingredients:

- 1 cup cooked quinoa
- 1 cup canned black beans, rinsed and drained
- 1 cup cherry tomatoes, halved
- 1/2 cup diced bell peppers
- 1/4 cup chopped fresh cilantro
- Juice of 1 lime
- 1 tablespoon olive oil
- Salt and pepper to taste

Directions:

1. In a large bowl, combine cooked quinoa, black beans, cherry tomatoes, bell peppers, and cilantro.
2. In a small bowl, whisk together lime juice, olive oil, salt, and pepper.
3. Pour the dressing over the salad and toss to combine.
4. Adjust the seasoning if needed.
5. Serve chilled and enjoy your quinoa and black bean salad!

Nutritional Information:

- Calories: 250
- Protein: 10g
- Carbohydrates: 35g
- Fat: 7g

Grilled Chicken and Vegetable Skewers

Ingredients:

- 2 boneless, skinless chicken breasts, cut into cubes
- 1 zucchini, sliced
- 1 bell pepper, cut into chunks
- 1 red onion, cut into wedges
- 2 tablespoons olive oil
- 2 cloves garlic, minced
- 1 teaspoon dried oregano
- Salt and pepper to taste

Directions:

1. Preheat the grill to medium-high heat.
2. In a bowl, combine olive oil, minced garlic, dried oregano, salt, and pepper.
3. Thread the chicken cubes, zucchini slices, bell pepper chunks, and red onion wedges onto skewers.
4. Brush the skewers with the olive oil mixture.
5. Place the skewers on the grill and cook for about 10-12 minutes, turning occasionally, until the chicken is cooked through and the vegetables are tender.
6. Remove from the grill and let them rest for a few minutes.
7. Serve the grilled chicken and vegetable skewers as a protein-packed side dish!

Nutritional Information:

- Calories: 280
- Protein: 30g
- Carbohydrates: 10g
- Fat: 14g

Baked Sweet Potato Fries

Ingredients:

- 2 large sweet potatoes, cut into fries
- 2 tablespoons olive oil
- 1 teaspoon paprika
- 1/2 teaspoon garlic powder
- 1/2 teaspoon salt
- 1/4 teaspoon black pepper

Directions:

1. Preheat the oven to 425°F (220°C) and line a baking sheet with parchment paper.
2. In a large bowl, toss the sweet potato fries with olive oil, paprika, garlic powder, salt, and black pepper until evenly coated.
3. Spread the fries in a single layer on the prepared baking sheet.
4. Bake for 25-30 minutes, flipping the fries halfway through, until they are crispy and golden brown.
5. Remove from the oven and let them cool slightly.
6. Serve the baked sweet potato fries as a delicious and healthy protein-rich side dish!

Nutritional Information:

- Calories: 180
- Protein: 3g
- Carbohydrates: 30g
- Fat: 6g

Greek Quinoa Salad

Ingredients:

- 1 cup cooked quinoa
- 1 cup diced cucumber
- 1 cup cherry tomatoes, halved
- 1/2 cup crumbled feta cheese
- 1/4 cup sliced Kalamata olives
- 1/4 cup diced red onion
- 2 tablespoons extra virgin olive oil
- 2 tablespoons lemon juice
- 1 teaspoon dried oregano
- Salt and pepper to taste

Directions:

1. In a large bowl, combine cooked quinoa, cucumber, cherry tomatoes, feta cheese, Kalamata olives, and red onion.
2. In a small bowl, whisk together olive oil, lemon juice, dried oregano, salt, and pepper.
3. Pour the dressing over the salad and toss to combine.
4. Adjust the seasoning if needed.
5. Refrigerate for at least 30 minutes to let the flavors meld.
6. Serve chilled and enjoy your Greek quinoa salad!

Nutritional Information:

- Calories: 290
- Protein: 12g
- Carbohydrates: 32g
- Fat: 14g

Roasted Brussels Sprouts
with Bacon

Ingredients:

- 1 pound Brussels sprouts, trimmed and halved
- 4 slices bacon, chopped
- 2 tablespoons olive oil
- 2 cloves garlic, minced
- Salt and pepper to taste

Directions:

1. Preheat the oven to 425°F (220°C) and line a baking sheet with parchment paper.
2. In a large bowl, toss the Brussels sprouts with chopped bacon, olive oil, minced garlic, salt, and pepper until well coated.
3. Spread the mixture in a single layer on the prepared baking sheet.
4. Roast in the oven for 20-25 minutes, stirring once or twice, until the Brussels sprouts are tender and browned.
5. Remove from the oven and let them cool slightly before serving.
6. Enjoy the flavorful and protein-packed roasted Brussels sprouts with bacon as a delightful side dish!

Nutritional Information:

- Calories: 180
- Protein: 8g
- Carbohydrates: 12g
- Fat: 12g

Quinoa and Chickpea Salad

Ingredients:

- 1 cup cooked quinoa
- 1 cup canned chickpeas, rinsed and drained
- 1 cup diced cucumber
- 1/2 cup diced red bell pepper
- 1/4 cup chopped fresh parsley
- 2 tablespoons lemon juice
- 2 tablespoons extra virgin olive oil
- 1 clove garlic, minced
- Salt and pepper to taste

Directions:

1. In a large bowl, combine cooked quinoa, chickpeas, cucumber, red bell pepper, and parsley.
2. In a small bowl, whisk together lemon juice, olive oil, minced garlic, salt, and pepper.
3. Pour the dressing over the salad and toss to combine.
4. Adjust the seasoning if needed.
5. Refrigerate for at least 30 minutes to let the flavors meld.
6. Serve chilled and enjoy your quinoa and chickpea salad!

Nutritional Information:

- Calories: 290
- Protein: 10g
- Carbohydrates: 40g
- Fat: 10g

Garlic Parmesan Roasted Brussels Sprouts

Ingredients:

- 1 pound Brussels sprouts, trimmed and halved
- 2 tablespoons olive oil
- 2 cloves garlic, minced
- 1/4 cup grated Parmesan cheese
- Salt and pepper to taste

Directions:

1. Preheat the oven to 425°F (220°C) and line a baking sheet with parchment paper.
2. In a large bowl, toss the Brussels sprouts with olive oil, minced garlic, salt, and pepper until well coated.
3. Spread the Brussels sprouts in a single layer on the prepared baking sheet.
4. Roast in the oven for 20-25 minutes, stirring once or twice, until the Brussels sprouts are tender and golden brown.
5. Remove from the oven and sprinkle grated Parmesan cheese over the Brussels sprouts.
6. Return to the oven for an additional 2-3 minutes until the cheese is melted and lightly browned.
7. Serve the garlic Parmesan roasted Brussels sprouts as a flavorful and protein-packed side dish!

Nutritional Information:

- Calories: 160
- Protein: 8g
- Carbohydrates: 12g
- Fat: 10g

Spicy Grilled Shrimp Skewers

Ingredients:

- 1 pound large shrimp, peeled and deveined
- 2 tablespoons olive oil
- 1 tablespoon lime juice
- 1 teaspoon chili powder
- 1/2 teaspoon smoked paprika
- 1/4 teaspoon cayenne pepper (adjust to taste)
- Salt and pepper to taste
- Wooden skewers, soaked in water

Directions:

1. Preheat the grill to medium-high heat.
2. In a bowl, combine olive oil, lime juice, chili powder, smoked paprika, cayenne pepper, salt, and pepper.
3. Thread the shrimp onto the soaked wooden skewers.
4. Brush the shrimp skewers with the olive oil mixture, coating them evenly.
5. Place the skewers on the grill and cook for about 2-3 minutes per side until the shrimp are opaque and cooked through.
6. Remove from the grill and let them rest for a few minutes.
7. Serve the spicy grilled shrimp skewers as a protein-rich and flavorful side dish!

Nutritional Information:

- Calories: 180
- Protein: 24g
- Carbohydrates: 2g
- Fat: 8g

Spinach and Feta Stuffed Mushrooms

Ingredients:

- 12 large mushrooms, stems removed
- 1 cup fresh spinach, chopped
- 1/2 cup crumbled feta cheese
- 2 tablespoons grated Parmesan cheese
- 2 tablespoons chopped fresh parsley
- 1 clove garlic, minced
- 2 tablespoons olive oil
- Salt and pepper to taste

Directions:

1. Preheat the oven to 375°F (190°C) and lightly grease a baking dish.
2. In a bowl, combine chopped spinach, feta cheese, Parmesan cheese, parsley, minced garlic, olive oil, salt, and pepper.
3. Spoon the spinach and feta mixture into the mushroom caps and place them in the prepared baking dish.
4. Bake for 15-20 minutes until the mushrooms are tender and the filling is golden brown.
5. Remove from the oven and let them cool slightly before serving.
6. Enjoy the delicious and protein-packed spinach and feta stuffed mushrooms as a flavorful side dish!

Nutritional Information:

- Calories: 120
- Protein: 6g
- Carbohydrates: 4g
- Fat: 9g

Quinoa and Kale Salad

Ingredients:

- 1 cup cooked quinoa
- 2 cups chopped kale
- 1/2 cup diced cucumber
- 1/2 cup cherry tomatoes, halved
- 1/4 cup chopped red onion
- 2 tablespoons lemon juice
- 2 tablespoons extra virgin olive oil
- 1 tablespoon Dijon mustard
- Salt and pepper to taste

Directions:

1. In a large bowl, combine cooked quinoa, chopped kale, diced cucumber, cherry tomatoes, and red onion.
2. In a small bowl, whisk together lemon juice, olive oil, Dijon mustard, salt, and pepper.
3. Pour the dressing over the salad and toss to combine.
4. Adjust the seasoning if needed.
5. Refrigerate for at least 30 minutes to allow the flavors to meld.
6. Serve chilled and enjoy your protein-packed quinoa and kale salad!

Nutritional Information:

- Calories: 220
- Protein: 9g
- Carbohydrates: 30g
- Fat: 8g

Garlic Roasted Green Beans

Ingredients:

- 1 pound fresh green beans, trimmed
- 2 tablespoons olive oil
- 2 cloves garlic, minced
- 1/2 teaspoon dried thyme
- Salt and pepper to taste

Directions:

1. Preheat the oven to 425°F (220°C) and line a baking sheet with parchment paper.
2. In a bowl, toss the green beans with olive oil, minced garlic, dried thyme, salt, and pepper until well coated.
3. Spread the green beans in a single layer on the prepared baking sheet.
4. Roast in the oven for 15-20 minutes, stirring once or twice, until the green beans are tender and slightly caramelized.
5. Remove from the oven and let them cool slightly before serving.
6. Enjoy the flavorful and protein-rich garlic roasted green beans as a delicious side dish!

Nutritional Information:

- Calories: 120
- Protein: 2g
- Carbohydrates: 10g
- Fat: 8g

Caprese Stuffed Avocado

Ingredients:

- 2 ripe avocados
- 1 cup cherry tomatoes, halved
- 1/2 cup fresh mozzarella balls, halved
- 2 tablespoons chopped fresh basil
- 1 tablespoon balsamic glaze
- Salt and pepper to taste

Directions:

1. Cut the avocados in half lengthwise and remove the pits.
2. Scoop out a bit of flesh from each avocado half to create a larger well.
3. In a bowl, combine cherry tomatoes, mozzarella balls, chopped basil, balsamic glaze, salt, and pepper.
4. Spoon the tomato and mozzarella mixture into the avocado halves, filling them generously.
5. Serve the caprese stuffed avocados as a protein-packed and refreshing side dish!

Nutritional Information:

- Calories: 250
- Protein: 8g
- Carbohydrates: 15g
- Fat: 20g

Quinoa and Black Bean Stuffed Bell Peppers

Ingredients:

- 4 bell peppers (any color)
- 1 cup cooked quinoa
- 1 cup canned black beans, rinsed and drained
- 1/2 cup diced tomatoes
- 1/2 cup corn kernels
- 1/4 cup diced red onion
- 1/4 cup shredded cheddar cheese
- 2 tablespoons chopped fresh cilantro
- 1 tablespoon olive oil
- 1 teaspoon cumin
- Salt and pepper to taste

Directions:

1. Preheat the oven to 375°F (190°C) and lightly grease a baking dish.
2. Cut the tops off the bell peppers and remove the seeds and membranes.
3. In a large bowl, combine cooked quinoa, black beans, diced tomatoes, corn kernels, red onion, shredded cheddar cheese, chopped cilantro, olive oil, cumin, salt, and pepper.
4. Spoon the quinoa and black bean mixture into the bell peppers and place them in the prepared baking dish.
5. Bake for 25-30 minutes until the peppers are tender and the filling is heated through.
6. Remove from the oven and let them cool for a few minutes before serving.
7. Enjoy the protein-packed and flavorful quinoa and black bean stuffed bell peppers!

Nutritional Information:

- Calories: 220
- Protein: 10g
- Carbohydrates: 35g
- Fat: 6g

Greek Yogurt Cucumber Salad

Ingredients:

- 2 cups diced cucumber
- 1 cup cherry tomatoes, halved
- 1/2 cup diced red onion
- 1/4 cup chopped fresh dill
- 1/4 cup chopped fresh mint
- 1/4 cup crumbled feta cheese
- 1/4 cup plain Greek yogurt
- 2 tablespoons lemon juice
- 1 tablespoon extra virgin olive oil
- Salt and pepper to taste

Directions:

1. In a large bowl, combine diced cucumber, cherry tomatoes, red onion, chopped dill, chopped mint, and crumbled feta cheese.
2. In a small bowl, whisk together Greek yogurt, lemon juice, olive oil, salt, and pepper.
3. Pour the dressing over the cucumber salad and toss to combine.
4. Adjust the seasoning if needed.
5. Refrigerate for at least 30 minutes to let the flavors meld.
6. Serve chilled and enjoy your protein-rich Greek yogurt cucumber salad!

Nutritional Information:

- Calories: 120
- Protein: 5g
- Carbohydrates: 10g
- Fat: 7g

Quinoa and Vegetable Stir-Fry

Ingredients:

- 1 cup cooked quinoa
- 1 cup mixed vegetables (such as bell peppers, broccoli, carrots)
- 1/2 cup sliced mushrooms
- 1/4 cup diced onion
- 2 cloves garlic, minced
- 2 tablespoons soy sauce
- 1 tablespoon sesame oil
- 1 tablespoon rice vinegar
- 1 teaspoon grated ginger
- Salt and pepper to taste

Directions:

1. In a large pan or wok, heat sesame oil over medium-high heat.
2. Add onions and garlic, and sauté until fragrant.
3. Add mixed vegetables and mushrooms, and stir-fry for a few minutes until they start to soften.
4. In a small bowl, whisk together soy sauce, rice vinegar, grated ginger, salt, and pepper.
5. Push the vegetables to one side of the pan and add the cooked quinoa to the other side.
6. Pour the sauce over the quinoa and vegetables, and stir everything together until well combined.
7. Cook for a few more minutes until heated through.

8. Serve the quinoa and vegetable stir-fry as a nutritious and protein-rich side dish!

Nutritional Information:

- Calories: 200
- Protein: 8g
- Carbohydrates: 30g
- Fat: 6g

◆

Roasted Sweet Potato Wedges

Ingredients:

- 2 large sweet potatoes, cut into wedges
- 2 tablespoons olive oil
- 1 teaspoon smoked paprika
- 1/2 teaspoon garlic powder
- 1/2 teaspoon dried rosemary
- Salt and pepper to taste

Directions:

1. Preheat the oven to 425°F (220°C) and line a baking sheet with parchment paper.
2. In a large bowl, toss the sweet potato wedges with olive oil, smoked paprika, garlic powder, dried rosemary, salt, and pepper until well coated.
3. Spread the wedges in a single layer on the prepared baking sheet.
4. Roast in the oven for 25-30 minutes, flipping once halfway through, until the sweet potatoes are tender and golden brown.
5. Remove from the oven and let them cool slightly before serving.

6. Enjoy the crispy and protein-packed roasted sweet potato wedges as a delicious side dish!

Nutritional Information:

- Calories: 180
- Protein: 2g
- Carbohydrates: 30g
- Fat: 6g

Greek Yogurt Coleslaw

Ingredients:

- 4 cups shredded cabbage
- 1 cup shredded carrots
- 1/2 cup plain Greek yogurt
- 2 tablespoons apple cider vinegar
- 1 tablespoon honey
- 1 teaspoon Dijon mustard
- 1/4 cup chopped fresh parsley
- Salt and pepper to taste

Directions:

1. In a large bowl, combine shredded cabbage and carrots.
2. In a small bowl, whisk together Greek yogurt, apple cider vinegar, honey, Dijon mustard, chopped parsley, salt, and pepper.
3. Pour the dressing over the cabbage mixture and toss to coat evenly.
4. Adjust the seasoning if needed.
5. Refrigerate for at least 30 minutes to let the flavors meld.
6. Serve chilled and enjoy your protein-rich Greek yogurt coleslaw!

Nutritional Information:

- Calories: 80
- Protein: 4g
- Carbohydrates: 12g
- Fat: 2g

Quinoa Salad

Ingredients:

- 1 cup quinoa
- 2 cups water
- 1 cucumber, chopped
- 1 bell pepper, chopped
- 1/4 cup feta cheese, crumbled
- 1/4 cup olive oil
- 2 tablespoons lemon juice
- Salt and pepper to taste

Directions:

1. Rinse the quinoa under cold water until the water runs clear.
2. In a pot, bring the water to a boil. Add the quinoa, reduce the heat to low, cover, and simmer for 15 minutes, or until the quinoa is tender.
3. In a large bowl, combine the cooked quinoa, cucumber, bell pepper, feta cheese, olive oil, lemon juice, salt, and pepper. Stir well to combine.
4. Serve the salad chilled or at room temperature.

Nutritional Values:

- Calories: 230

- Protein: 8g
- Fat: 10g
- Carbs: 30g

❖

Chickpea and Spinach Stir-fry

Ingredients:

- 2 cups cooked chickpeas
- 2 cups fresh spinach
- 2 cloves garlic, minced
- 1 tablespoon olive oil
- Salt and pepper to taste

Directions:

1. Heat the olive oil in a pan over medium heat.
2. Add the garlic and sauté until fragrant.
3. Add the chickpeas and spinach to the pan. Cook until the spinach is wilted and the chickpeas are heated through.
4. Season with salt and pepper to taste.

Nutritional Values:

- Calories: 250
- Protein: 12g
- Fat: 6g
- Carbs: 40g

❖

Broccoli and Tofu Stir-Fry

Ingredients:

- 1 cup tofu, cubed
- 2 cups broccoli florets
- 1 tablespoon soy sauce
- 1 tablespoon sesame oil
- 1 clove garlic, minced

Directions:

1. Heat the sesame oil in a pan over medium heat.
2. Add the garlic and sauté until fragrant.
3. Add the tofu and broccoli to the pan. Cook for about 5 minutes, or until the tofu is golden and the broccoli is tender.
4. Drizzle with soy sauce and stir to combine.

Nutritional Values:

- Calories: 210
- Protein: 15g
- Fat: 10g
- Carbs: 20g

Black Bean and Corn Salad

Ingredients:

- 2 cups black beans, cooked
- 1 cup corn kernels
- 1/2 cup red onion, chopped
- 1 bell pepper, chopped

- 2 tablespoons lime juice
- 1 tablespoon olive oil
- Salt and pepper to taste

Directions:

1. In a large bowl, combine the black beans, corn, red onion, and bell pepper.
2. Drizzle with the lime juice and olive oil.
3. Season with salt and pepper to taste, and stir well to combine.
4. Serve chilled or at room temperature.

Nutritional Values:

- Calories: 200
- Protein: 11g
- Fat: 4g
- Carbs: 36g

Roasted Brussels Sprouts with Almonds

Ingredients:

- 2 cups Brussels sprouts, halved
- 1/4 cup almonds, chopped
- 2 tablespoons olive oil
- Salt and pepper to taste

Directions:

1. Preheat your oven to 400°F (200°C).

2. Toss the Brussels sprouts with the olive oil, salt, and pepper, and spread them out on a baking sheet.
3. Roast for 20 minutes, or until the Brussels sprouts are tender and golden.
4. Sprinkle with the chopped almonds before serving.

Nutritional Values:

- Calories: 180
- Protein: 6g
- Fat: 12g
- Carbs: 16g

Cauliflower "Rice" Pilaf

Ingredients:

- 1 head cauliflower, riced
- 1 onion, chopped
- 2 cloves garlic, minced
- 2 tablespoons olive oil
- Salt and pepper to taste

Directions:

1. Heat the olive oil in a pan over medium heat.
2. Add the onion and garlic, and sauté until fragrant.
3. Add the riced cauliflower, salt, and pepper. Cook for about 5 minutes, or until the cauliflower is tender.
4. Serve hot.

Nutritional Values:

- Calories: 120
- Protein: 4g

- Fat: 7g
- Carbs: 13g

Lentil and Carrot Salad

Ingredients:

- 2 cups lentils, cooked
- 2 carrots, shredded
- 1/4 cup parsley, chopped
- 2 tablespoons lemon juice
- 1 tablespoon olive oil
- Salt and pepper to taste

Directions:

1. In a large bowl, combine the lentils and shredded carrot.
2. Drizzle with the lemon juice and olive oil.
3. Season with salt and pepper, and stir in the chopped parsley.
4. Serve chilled or at room temperature.

Nutritional Values:

- Calories: 240
- Protein: 18g
- Fat: 3g
- Carbs: 40g

VEGETABLES

Chickpea and Vegetable Salad

Ingredients:

- 1 can of chickpeas
- 1 cucumber, diced
- 1 tomato, diced
- 1 red bell pepper, diced
- 1 red onion, thinly sliced
- 1 handful of fresh parsley, chopped
- Juice of 1 lemon
- 2 tablespoons of olive oil
- Salt and pepper to taste

Directions:

1. Drain and rinse the chickpeas under cold water.
2. In a large bowl, combine the chickpeas, cucumber, tomato, bell pepper, red onion, and parsley.
3. In a small bowl, mix together the lemon juice, olive oil, salt, and pepper.
4. Pour the dressing over the vegetables and gently toss until all the ingredients are well coated.
5. Serve the chickpea and vegetable salad as a main dish or as a side dish.

Nutritional values (per serving):

- Calories: 220
- Protein: 10g
- Fat: 8g
- Carbohydrates: 28g
- Fiber: 8g

Lentil and Vegetable Soup

Ingredients:

- 1 cup of red lentils
- 2 carrots, sliced
- 2 celery stalks, diced
- 1 onion, chopped
- 2 garlic cloves, minced
- 4 cups of vegetable broth
- 1 teaspoon of turmeric
- 1 teaspoon of smoked paprika
- Salt and pepper to taste
- Fresh parsley, chopped (for garnish)

Directions:

1. In a large pot, sauté the onion and garlic with a little olive oil until lightly golden.
2. Add the carrots, celery, and lentils. Stir for a few minutes.
3. Add the vegetable broth, turmeric, smoked paprika, salt, and pepper. Bring to a boil, then reduce the heat and let it simmer for about 20-25 minutes or until the lentils are tender.
4. Blend half of the soup with an immersion blender to achieve a creamy consistency.
5. Serve the lentil and vegetable soup hot, garnished with fresh parsley.

Nutritional values (per serving):

- Calories: 250
- Protein: 14g
- Fat: 2g
- Carbohydrates: 46g
- Fiber: 14g

Grilled Portobello Mushroom Burger

Ingredients:

- 2 large Portobello mushrooms
- 1 tablespoon of balsamic vinegar
- 2 tablespoons of soy sauce
- 2 tablespoons of olive oil
- 2 whole wheat burger buns
- 2 slices of tomato
- 2 lettuce leaves
- Optional toppings: sliced avocado, red onion, mustard, or vegan cheese

Directions:

1. Preheat the grill or grill pan to medium heat.
2. In a small bowl, whisk together the balsamic vinegar, soy sauce, and olive oil.
3. Clean the Portobello mushrooms and remove the stems.
4. Brush the mushroom caps with the marinade on both sides.
5. Place the mushrooms on the grill and cook for about 4-5 minutes per side or until tender.
6. Toast the burger buns on the grill for a minute or two.
7. Assemble the burger by placing a grilled mushroom on the bottom half of each bun.
8. Top with a slice of tomato, lettuce leaf, and any desired toppings.
9. Cover with the top bun and serve the grilled Portobello mushroom burger.

Nutritional values (per serving):

- Calories: 180
- Protein: 8g
- Fat: 7g

- Carbohydrates: 23g
- Fiber: 4g

◆

Grilled Eggplant with Yogurt Sauce

Ingredients:

- 1 large eggplant
- 2 tablespoons of olive oil
- 1 teaspoon of paprika
- Salt and pepper to taste
- 1 cup of plain Greek yogurt
- 1 clove of garlic, minced
- Juice of 1 lemon
- Fresh herbs for garnish (e.g., mint or parsley)

Directions:

1. Preheat the grill or grill pan to medium-high heat.
2. Slice the eggplant into rounds, about 1/2-inch thick.
3. In a small bowl, mix together the olive oil, paprika, salt, and pepper.
4. Brush both sides of the eggplant slices with the oil mixture.
5. Grill the eggplant for about 3-4 minutes per side, or until tender and grill marks appear.
6. In another bowl, combine the Greek yogurt, minced garlic, lemon juice, salt, and pepper.
7. Serve the grilled eggplant with a dollop of yogurt sauce on top.
8. Garnish with fresh herbs and enjoy!

Nutritional values (per serving):

- Calories: 150

- Protein: 8g
- Fat: 10g
- Carbohydrates: 12g
- Fiber: 5g

❖

Baked Stuffed Zucchini Boats

Ingredients:

- 2 medium zucchini
- 1 cup of cooked quinoa
- 1/2 cup of diced bell peppers
- 1/2 cup of diced tomatoes
- 1/2 cup of cooked black beans
- 1/4 cup of chopped red onion
- 1/4 cup of shredded cheddar cheese (optional)
- 1 teaspoon of dried oregano
- Salt and pepper to taste

Directions:

1. Preheat the oven to 375°F (190°C).
2. Cut the zucchini in half lengthwise and scoop out the flesh, leaving a hollow shell.
3. In a mixing bowl, combine the cooked quinoa, diced bell peppers, diced tomatoes, cooked black beans, red onion, dried oregano, salt, and pepper.
4. Fill the zucchini boats with the quinoa mixture, pressing it down lightly.
5. Place the stuffed zucchini boats on a baking sheet and bake for about 20 minutes.
6. If desired, sprinkle shredded cheddar cheese on top and bake for an additional 5 minutes until melted.
7. Serve the baked stuffed zucchini boats as a protein-rich and flavorful meal.

Nutritional values (per serving):

- Calories: 220
- Protein: 10g
- Fat: 4g
- Carbohydrates: 36g
- Fiber: 8g

Baked Stuffed Bell Peppers

Ingredients:

- 4 bell peppers (any color)
- 1 cup of cooked quinoa
- 1 cup of cooked lentils
- 1 small onion, diced
- 2 cloves of garlic, minced
- 1 cup of diced tomatoes
- 1 teaspoon of dried basil
- 1 teaspoon of dried oregano
- Salt and pepper to taste
- Optional: shredded cheese for topping

Directions:

1. Preheat the oven to 375°F (190°C).
2. Cut off the tops of the bell peppers and remove the seeds and membranes.
3. In a skillet, sauté the onion and garlic until translucent.
4. Add the cooked quinoa, lentils, diced tomatoes, dried basil, dried oregano, salt, and pepper to the skillet. Stir well to combine.
5. Fill each bell pepper with the quinoa and lentil mixture.
6. If desired, sprinkle shredded cheese on top of each pepper.

7. Place the stuffed bell peppers in a baking dish and bake for about 25-30 minutes or until the peppers are tender and the cheese is melted and bubbly.
8. Remove from the oven and let them cool slightly before serving.

Nutritional values (per serving):

- Calories: 250
- Protein: 15g
- Fat: 5g
- Carbohydrates: 40g
- Fiber: 10g

Grilled Asparagus with Lemon and Parmesan

Ingredients:

- 1 bunch of asparagus
- 1 tablespoon of olive oil
- Zest of 1 lemon
- Juice of 1 lemon
- 1/4 cup of grated Parmesan cheese
- Salt and pepper to taste

Directions:

1. Preheat the grill or grill pan to medium-high heat.
2. Trim off the tough ends of the asparagus spears.
3. In a shallow dish, combine the olive oil, lemon zest, lemon juice, salt, and pepper.
4. Place the asparagus in the dish and toss to coat evenly with the mixture.

5. Grill the asparagus for about 3-5 minutes, turning occasionally, until tender and lightly charred.
6. Remove the asparagus from the grill and sprinkle with grated Parmesan cheese.
7. Serve the grilled asparagus as a delicious and nutritious side dish.

Nutritional values (per serving):

- Calories: 90
- Protein: 6g
- Fat: 6g
- Carbohydrates: 6g
- Fiber: 3g

Quinoa and Chickpea Salad

Ingredients:

- 1 cup of cooked quinoa
- 1 can of chickpeas, drained and rinsed
- 1 cup of cherry tomatoes, halved
- 1 cucumber, diced
- 1 bell pepper, diced
- 1/4 cup of chopped red onion
- 1/4 cup of chopped fresh parsley
- Juice of 1 lemon
- 2 tablespoons of olive oil
- Salt and pepper to taste

Directions:

1. In a large bowl, combine the cooked quinoa, chickpeas, cherry tomatoes, cucumber, bell pepper, red onion, and parsley.

2. In a small bowl, whisk together the lemon juice, olive oil, salt, and pepper.
3. Pour the dressing over the quinoa mixture and toss to coat all the ingredients evenly.
4. Adjust the seasoning if needed.
5. Serve the quinoa and chickpea salad as a refreshing and protein-packed meal.

Nutritional values (per serving):

- Calories: 280
- Protein: 10g
- Fat: 8g
- Carbohydrates: 42g
- Fiber: 8g

Roasted Cauliflower Steaks with Tahini Sauce

Ingredients:

- 1 large head of cauliflower
- 2 tablespoons of olive oil
- 1 teaspoon of paprika
- Salt and pepper to taste
- 1/4 cup of tahini
- 2 tablespoons of lemon juice
- 1 clove of garlic, minced
- Water (as needed to thin the sauce)
- Optional toppings: chopped parsley, pomegranate seeds

Directions:

1. Preheat the oven to 400°F (200°C).

2. Trim off the leaves and the bottom stem of the cauliflower, keeping the head intact.
3. Slice the cauliflower vertically into 1-inch thick steaks.
4. In a small bowl, mix together the olive oil, paprika, salt, and pepper.
5. Brush both sides of the cauliflower steaks with the oil mixture and place them on a baking sheet.
6. Roast the cauliflower in the preheated oven for about 20-25 minutes or until golden brown and tender.
7. In another bowl, whisk together the tahini, lemon juice, minced garlic, and water until smooth and creamy. Add water gradually until desired consistency is reached.
8. Serve the roasted cauliflower steaks with a drizzle of tahini sauce.
9. Garnish with chopped parsley and pomegranate seeds, if desired.

Nutritional values (per serving):

- Calories: 180
- Protein: 6g
- Fat: 14g
- Carbohydrates: 12g
- Fiber: 5g

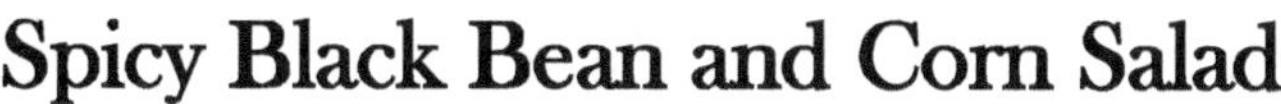

Spicy Black Bean and Corn Salad

Ingredients:

- 1 can of black beans, drained and rinsed
- 1 cup of corn kernels (fresh or frozen)
- 1 bell pepper, diced
- 1 small red onion, diced
- 1 jalapeño pepper, seeded and minced
- Juice of 1 lime

- 2 tablespoons of olive oil
- 1 teaspoon of cumin
- 1/2 teaspoon of chili powder
- Salt and pepper to taste
- Fresh cilantro for garnish

Directions:

1. In a large bowl, combine the black beans, corn kernels, bell pepper, red onion, and jalapeño pepper.
2. In a small bowl, whisk together the lime juice, olive oil, cumin, chili powder, salt, and pepper.
3. Pour the dressing over the black bean mixture and toss to coat.
4. Adjust the seasoning if needed.
5. Let the salad sit for at least 30 minutes to allow the flavors to meld together.
6. Garnish with fresh cilantro before serving.

Nutritional values (per serving):

- Calories: 180
- Protein: 8g
- Fat: 6g
- Carbohydrates: 26g
- Fiber: 8g

Broccoli and Quinoa Casserole

Ingredients:

- 1 cup of cooked quinoa
- 2 cups of broccoli florets
- 1 small onion, diced
- 2 cloves of garlic, minced

- 1 cup of shredded cheddar cheese
- 1/2 cup of plain Greek yogurt
- 1/4 cup of grated Parmesan cheese
- 2 tablespoons of olive oil
- Salt and pepper to taste

Directions:

1. Preheat the oven to 375°F (190°C).
2. In a large skillet, heat the olive oil over medium heat.
3. Sauté the onion and garlic until translucent.
4. Add the broccoli florets to the skillet and cook until tender-crisp.
5. In a mixing bowl, combine the cooked quinoa, sautéed vegetables, shredded cheddar cheese, Greek yogurt, salt, and pepper.
6. Transfer the mixture to a greased casserole dish.
7. Sprinkle the grated Parmesan cheese on top.
8. Bake in the preheated oven for about 20-25 minutes or until the casserole is heated through and the cheese is melted and bubbly.
9. Let it cool for a few minutes before serving.

Nutritional values (per serving):

- Calories: 280
- Protein: 14g
- Fat: 16g
- Carbohydrates: 22g
- Fiber: 4g

Chickpea and Vegetable Curry

Ingredients:

- 1 can of chickpeas, drained and rinsed
- 1 onion, diced
- 2 cloves of garlic, minced
- 1 bell pepper, diced
- 1 zucchini, diced
- 1 cup of diced tomatoes
- 1 cup of coconut milk
- 2 tablespoons of curry powder
- 1 tablespoon of olive oil
- Salt and pepper to taste
- Fresh cilantro for garnish

Directions:

1. In a large skillet, heat the olive oil over medium heat.
2. Sauté the onion and garlic until translucent.
3. Add the bell pepper and zucchini to the skillet and cook until tender.
4. Stir in the diced tomatoes, chickpeas, curry powder, salt, and pepper.
5. Pour in the coconut milk and simmer for about 10 minutes to allow the flavors to meld together.
6. Adjust the seasoning if needed.
7. Serve the chickpea and vegetable curry over rice or with naan bread.
8. Garnish with fresh cilantro before serving.

Nutritional values (per serving):

- Calories: 280
- Protein: 10g
- Fat: 12g
- Carbohydrates: 38g
- Fiber: 8g

Greek-style Stuffed Eggplant

Ingredients:

- 2 medium eggplants
- 1 cup of cooked quinoa
- 1 cup of diced tomatoes
- 1/2 cup of diced cucumber
- 1/4 cup of chopped red onion
- 1/4 cup of crumbled feta cheese
- 2 tablespoons of chopped fresh parsley
- 2 tablespoons of lemon juice
- 2 tablespoons of olive oil
- Salt and pepper to taste

Directions:

1. Preheat the oven to 400°F (200°C).
2. Cut the eggplants in half lengthwise and scoop out the flesh, leaving a hollow shell.
3. Brush the eggplant shells with olive oil and place them on a baking sheet.
4. Bake in the preheated oven for about 15-20 minutes or until the eggplant is tender.
5. In a mixing bowl, combine the cooked quinoa, diced tomatoes, cucumber, red onion, feta cheese, parsley, lemon juice, olive oil, salt, and pepper.
6. Fill each eggplant shell with the quinoa mixture.
7. Return the stuffed eggplants to the oven and bake for an additional 10 minutes.
8. Serve the Greek-style stuffed eggplant as a flavorful and protein-rich meal.

Nutritional values (per serving):

- Calories: 230
- Protein: 8g
- Fat: 10g

- Carbohydrates: 30g
- Fiber: 10g

---◆---

Grilled Tofu and Vegetable Skewers

Ingredients:

- 1 block of firm tofu, pressed and cut into cubes
- 1 zucchini, cut into thick slices
- 1 bell pepper, cut into chunks
- 1 red onion, cut into wedges
- 8 cherry tomatoes
- 2 tablespoons of olive oil
- 2 tablespoons of soy sauce
- 1 tablespoon of maple syrup
- 1 teaspoon of garlic powder
- Salt and pepper to taste

Directions:

1. In a small bowl, whisk together the olive oil, soy sauce, maple syrup, garlic powder, salt, and pepper to make the marinade.
2. Thread the tofu cubes and vegetables onto skewers, alternating between different ingredients.
3. Place the skewers in a shallow dish and pour the marinade over them, ensuring they are evenly coated.
4. Let the skewers marinate for at least 30 minutes to allow the flavors to develop.
5. Preheat the grill to medium-high heat.
6. Grill the tofu and vegetable skewers for about 10-12 minutes, turning occasionally, until the tofu is lightly charred and the vegetables are tender.
7. Serve the grilled tofu and vegetable skewers as a protein-packed and flavorful dish.

Nutritional values (per serving):

- Calories: 200
- Protein: 12g
- Fat: 10g
- Carbohydrates: 18g
- Fiber: 4g

Lentil and Vegetable Stir-Fry

Ingredients:

- 1 cup of cooked lentils
- 1 cup of mixed vegetables (e.g., broccoli, carrots, snow peas)
- 1 bell pepper, sliced
- 1 small onion, sliced
- 2 cloves of garlic, minced
- 2 tablespoons of low-sodium soy sauce
- 1 tablespoon of sesame oil
- 1 teaspoon of grated ginger
- Salt and pepper to taste

Directions:

1. Heat the sesame oil in a large skillet or wok over medium-high heat.
2. Add the garlic and grated ginger to the skillet and sauté until fragrant.
3. Add the mixed vegetables, bell pepper, and onion to the skillet. Stir-fry for a few minutes until the vegetables are tender-crisp.
4. Stir in the cooked lentils and continue to cook for another 2-3 minutes to heat through.

5. Pour in the soy sauce and season with salt and pepper. Stir well to coat all the ingredients.
6. Cook for an additional 1-2 minutes to allow the flavors to meld together.
7. Serve the lentil and vegetable stir-fry as a nutritious and protein-rich meal.

Nutritional values (per serving):

- Calories: 220
- Protein: 12g
- Fat: 6g
- Carbohydrates: 32g
- Fiber: 10g

Roasted Brussels Sprouts and Quinoa Salad

Ingredients:

- 1 cup of cooked quinoa
- 2 cups of Brussels sprouts, halved
- 1 tablespoon of olive oil
- 2 cloves of garlic, minced
- 1/4 cup of dried cranberries
- 1/4 cup of chopped walnuts
- Juice of 1 lemon
- Salt and pepper to taste

Directions:

1. Preheat the oven to 400°F (200°C).
2. Toss the Brussels sprouts with olive oil, minced garlic, salt, and pepper.

3. Spread the Brussels sprouts on a baking sheet and roast for about 20 minutes or until crispy and browned.
4. In a large bowl, combine the cooked quinoa, roasted Brussels sprouts, dried cranberries, chopped walnuts, lemon juice, salt, and pepper.
5. Toss to mix well and adjust the seasoning if needed.
6. Serve the roasted Brussels sprouts and quinoa salad as a nutritious and protein-packed meal.

Nutritional values (per serving):

- Calories: 280
- Protein: 11g
- Fat: 12g
- Carbohydrates: 36g
- Fiber: 7g

Grilled Eggplant with Chickpea Salad

Ingredients:

- 1 large eggplant
- 1 can of chickpeas, drained and rinsed
- 1 cup of cherry tomatoes, halved
- 1/4 cup of chopped red onion
- 2 tablespoons of fresh lemon juice
- 2 tablespoons of olive oil
- 1 clove of garlic, minced
- Salt and pepper to taste
- Fresh parsley for garnish

Directions:

1. Preheat the grill to medium heat.
2. Slice the eggplant into rounds, about 1/2-inch thick.

3. In a small bowl, whisk together the lemon juice, olive oil, minced garlic, salt, and pepper.
4. Brush both sides of the eggplant slices with the dressing.
5. Grill the eggplant for about 4-5 minutes per side, until tender and lightly charred.
6. In a separate bowl, combine the chickpeas, cherry tomatoes, red onion, and fresh parsley.
7. Drizzle the remaining dressing over the salad and toss to combine.
8. Serve the grilled eggplant with a side of the chickpea salad.

Nutritional values (per serving):

- Calories: 180
- Protein: 8g
- Fat: 7g
- Carbohydrates: 23g
- Fiber: 7g

Quinoa Stuffed Bell Peppers

Ingredients:

- 4 bell peppers (any color)
- 1 cup of cooked quinoa
- 1 cup of black beans, drained and rinsed
- 1 cup of diced tomatoes
- 1/2 cup of corn kernels
- 1/4 cup of diced red onion
- 1/4 cup of chopped fresh cilantro
- 1 tablespoon of lime juice
- 1 teaspoon of ground cumin
- Salt and pepper to taste

Directions:

1. Preheat the oven to 375°F (190°C).
2. Cut off the tops of the bell peppers and remove the seeds and membranes.
3. In a large bowl, combine the cooked quinoa, black beans, diced tomatoes, corn kernels, red onion, cilantro, lime juice, ground cumin, salt, and pepper. Mix well.
4. Stuff the bell peppers with the quinoa mixture, pressing it down lightly.
5. Place the stuffed bell peppers in a baking dish and cover with foil.
6. Bake for 30-35 minutes, until the peppers are tender and the filling is heated through.
7. Serve the quinoa stuffed bell peppers as a protein-rich and satisfying meal.

Nutritional values (per serving):

- Calories: 220
- Protein: 10g
- Fat: 2g
- Carbohydrates: 46g
- Fiber: 10g

Lentil and Vegetable Curry

Ingredients:

- 1 cup of dried lentils
- 1 onion, diced
- 2 cloves of garlic, minced
- 1 tablespoon of grated ginger
- 1 can of diced tomatoes
- 2 cups of vegetable broth

- 2 cups of fresh spinach leaves
- 1 tablespoon of curry powder
- 1 teaspoon of ground cumin
- 1 teaspoon of ground coriander
- Salt and pepper to taste
- Optional toppings: chopped cilantro, yogurt

Directions:

1. Rinse the lentils under cold water and drain.
2. In a large pot, sauté the onion, garlic, and ginger until fragrant and translucent.
3. Add the lentils, diced tomatoes, vegetable broth, curry powder, cumin, coriander, salt, and pepper to the pot.
4. Bring the mixture to a boil, then reduce the heat and simmer for about 20-25 minutes or until the lentils are tender.
5. Stir in the spinach leaves and cook until wilted.
6. Adjust the seasoning if needed.
7. Serve the lentil and vegetable curry over rice or with naan bread.
8. Garnish with chopped cilantro and a dollop of yogurt, if desired.

Nutritional values (per serving):

- Calories: 250
- Protein: 15g
- Fat: 2g
- Carbohydrates: 45g
- Fiber: 15g

Broccoli and Chickpea Salad

Ingredients:

- 2 cups of broccoli florets
- 1 can of chickpeas, drained and rinsed
- 1/4 cup of diced red onion
- 1/4 cup of chopped fresh parsley
- 2 tablespoons of lemon juice
- 2 tablespoons of olive oil
- 1 clove of garlic, minced
- Salt and pepper to taste

Directions:

1. Steam the broccoli florets until crisp-tender. Let them cool.
2. In a large bowl, combine the steamed broccoli, chickpeas, diced red onion, and chopped parsley.
3. In a small bowl, whisk together the lemon juice, olive oil, minced garlic, salt, and pepper.
4. Pour the dressing over the salad and toss to coat all the ingredients.
5. Adjust the seasoning if needed.
6. Let the salad sit for at least 30 minutes to allow the flavors to meld together.
7. Serve the broccoli and chickpea salad as a protein-packed and nutritious side dish.

Nutritional values (per serving):

- Calories: 220
- Protein: 10g
- Fat: 10g
- Carbohydrates: 26g
- Fiber: 8g

Zucchini Noodles with Tofu and Peanut Sauce

Ingredients:

- 2 medium zucchinis
- 1 block of tofu, pressed and cubed
- 2 tablespoons of peanut butter
- 2 tablespoons of soy sauce
- 1 tablespoon of rice vinegar
- 1 tablespoon of maple syrup
- 1 clove of garlic, minced
- 1/2 teaspoon of grated ginger
- 1 tablespoon of sesame oil
- 2 tablespoons of chopped peanuts (for garnish)
- Fresh cilantro (for garnish)

Directions:

1. Use a spiralizer or a vegetable peeler to create zucchini noodles.
2. In a large non-stick skillet, heat the sesame oil over medium heat.
3. Add the tofu cubes to the skillet and cook until golden brown on all sides. Set aside.
4. In a small bowl, whisk together the peanut butter, soy sauce, rice vinegar, maple syrup, minced garlic, and grated ginger to make the sauce.
5. In the same skillet, add the zucchini noodles and cook for 2-3 minutes until slightly softened.
6. Add the tofu back to the skillet and pour the peanut sauce over the noodles and tofu.
7. Stir gently to coat the noodles and tofu in the sauce and cook for an additional 2-3 minutes.
8. Serve the zucchini noodles with tofu and peanut sauce garnished with chopped peanuts and fresh cilantro.

Nutritional values (per serving):

- Calories: 320
- Protein: 18g
- Fat: 20g
- Carbohydrates: 24g
- Fiber: 6g

Spaghetti Squash with Lentil Bolognese

Ingredients:

- 1 large spaghetti squash
- 1 cup of cooked lentils
- 1 can of crushed tomatoes
- 1 small onion, diced
- 2 cloves of garlic, minced
- 1 carrot, diced
- 1 celery stalk, diced
- 1 tablespoon of olive oil
- 1 teaspoon of dried oregano
- 1 teaspoon of dried basil
- Salt and pepper to taste
- Fresh basil leaves (for garnish)

Directions:

1. Preheat the oven to 400°F (200°C).
2. Cut the spaghetti squash in half lengthwise and remove the seeds.
3. Place the squash halves cut-side down on a baking sheet and roast in the oven for 40-45 minutes, or until the flesh is easily scraped with a fork.
4. In a large skillet, heat the olive oil over medium heat.

5. Add the diced onion, minced garlic, diced carrot, and diced celery to the skillet. Sauté until the vegetables are tender.
6. Stir in the cooked lentils, crushed tomatoes, dried oregano, dried basil, salt, and pepper. Simmer for 15-20 minutes to allow the flavors to meld together.
7. Once the spaghetti squash is cooked, scrape the flesh with a fork to create "noodles."
8. Serve the spaghetti squash topped with the lentil bolognese sauce.
9. Garnish with fresh basil leaves.

Nutritional values (per serving):

- Calories: 240
- Protein: 12g
- Fat: 4g
- Carbohydrates: 44g
- Fiber: 10g

MEAT

Grilled Chicken Breast with Lemon-Herb Marinade

Ingredients:

- 2 boneless, skinless chicken breasts
- Juice of 1 lemon
- 2 tablespoons of olive oil
- 2 cloves of garlic, minced
- 1 tablespoon of chopped fresh herbs (such as rosemary, thyme, or parsley)
- Salt and pepper to taste

Directions:

1. In a bowl, whisk together the lemon juice, olive oil, minced garlic, chopped herbs, salt, and pepper to make the marinade.
2. Place the chicken breasts in a shallow dish and pour the marinade over them, ensuring they are evenly coated.
3. Let the chicken marinate for at least 30 minutes or up to overnight in the refrigerator.
4. Preheat the grill to medium-high heat.
5. Remove the chicken from the marinade and discard the remaining marinade.
6. Grill the chicken breasts for about 6-8 minutes per side, or until cooked through and no longer pink in the center.
7. Let the chicken rest for a few minutes before serving.

Nutritional values (per serving):

- Calories: 220
- Protein: 28g
- Fat: 10g
- Carbohydrates: 1g
- Fiber: 0g

Grilled Steak with Chimichurri Sauce

Ingredients:

- 2 boneless beef steaks (such as ribeye or sirloin)
- Salt and pepper to taste

For the chimichurri sauce:

- 1 cup of fresh parsley leaves
- 1/4 cup of fresh cilantro leaves
- 2 cloves of garlic
- 1/4 cup of red wine vinegar
- 1/2 cup of olive oil
- 1 teaspoon of dried oregano
- Salt and pepper to taste

Directions:

1. Preheat the grill to high heat.
2. Season the steaks with salt and pepper on both sides.
3. Grill the steaks for about 4-6 minutes per side, or until desired doneness.
4. While the steaks are grilling, prepare the chimichurri sauce. In a food processor or blender, combine the parsley, cilantro, garlic, red wine vinegar, olive oil, dried oregano, salt, and pepper. Pulse until well combined but still slightly chunky.
5. Remove the steaks from the grill and let them rest for a few minutes.
6. Slice the steaks against the grain and serve with a drizzle of chimichurri sauce on top.

Nutritional values (per serving):

- Calories: 400
- Protein: 40g
- Fat: 26g

- Carbohydrates: 2g
- Fiber: 1g

Baked Chicken Breast with Herbs

Ingredients:

- 2 boneless, skinless chicken breasts
- 2 tablespoons of olive oil
- 1 teaspoon of dried thyme
- 1 teaspoon of dried rosemary
- 1 teaspoon of dried oregano
- Salt and pepper to taste

Directions:

1. Preheat the oven to 400°F (200°C).
2. In a small bowl, mix together the olive oil, dried thyme, dried rosemary, dried oregano, salt, and pepper to make a herb marinade.
3. Place the chicken breasts in a baking dish and brush the herb marinade over them, ensuring they are evenly coated.
4. Bake the chicken breasts in the preheated oven for about 20-25 minutes, or until cooked through and no longer pink in the center.
5. Let the chicken rest for a few minutes before serving.

Nutritional values (per serving):

- Calories: 200
- Protein: 30g
- Fat: 9g
- Carbohydrates: 0g
- Fiber: 0g

Pork Tenderloin with Mustard Glaze

Ingredients:

- 1 pound of pork tenderloin
- 2 tablespoons of Dijon mustard
- 1 tablespoon of honey
- 1 tablespoon of olive oil
- 1 teaspoon of dried thyme
- Salt and pepper to taste

Directions:

1. Preheat the oven to 375°F (190°C).
2. In a small bowl, whisk together the Dijon mustard, honey, olive oil, dried thyme, salt, and pepper to make the mustard glaze.
3. Place the pork tenderloin in a baking dish and brush the mustard glaze over it, ensuring it is evenly coated.
4. Bake the pork tenderloin in the preheated oven for about 25-30 minutes, or until the internal temperature reaches 145°F (63°C).
5. Remove the pork from the oven and let it rest for a few minutes before slicing.

Nutritional values (per serving):

- Calories: 250
- Protein: 35g
- Fat: 10

Grilled Lemon Herb Chicken Thighs

Ingredients:

- 4 bone-in, skin-on chicken thighs
- Juice of 1 lemon
- 2 tablespoons of olive oil
- 2 cloves of garlic, minced
- 1 tablespoon of chopped fresh herbs (such as rosemary, thyme, or parsley)
- Salt and pepper to taste

Directions:

1. In a bowl, whisk together the lemon juice, olive oil, minced garlic, chopped herbs, salt, and pepper to make the marinade.
2. Place the chicken thighs in a shallow dish and pour the marinade over them, ensuring they are evenly coated.
3. Let the chicken marinate for at least 30 minutes or up to overnight in the refrigerator.
4. Preheat the grill to medium-high heat.
5. Remove the chicken from the marinade and discard the remaining marinade.
6. Grill the chicken thighs for about 6-8 minutes per side, or until cooked through and the internal temperature reaches 165°F (74°C).
7. Let the chicken rest for a few minutes before serving.

Nutritional values (per serving):

- Calories: 300
- Protein: 26g
- Fat: 20g
- Carbohydrates: 2g
- Fiber: 0g

Beef Stir-Fry with Broccoli and Bell Peppers

Ingredients:

- 1 pound of beef sirloin, thinly sliced
- 2 cups of broccoli florets
- 1 bell pepper, thinly sliced
- 1 small onion, thinly sliced
- 2 cloves of garlic, minced
- 2 tablespoons of low-sodium soy sauce
- 1 tablespoon of oyster sauce
- 1 tablespoon of cornstarch
- 1 tablespoon of vegetable oil
- Salt and pepper to taste

Directions:

1. In a small bowl, whisk together the soy sauce, oyster sauce, cornstarch, salt, and pepper to make the sauce.
2. In a large skillet or wok, heat the vegetable oil over high heat.
3. Add the minced garlic and stir-fry for about 30 seconds until fragrant.
4. Add the beef slices to the skillet and stir-fry for 2-3 minutes until browned. Remove from the skillet and set aside.
5. In the same skillet, add the broccoli florets, bell pepper slices, and onion slices. Stir-fry for 3-4 minutes until the vegetables are crisp-tender.
6. Return the beef to the skillet and pour the sauce over the stir-fry.
7. Stir well to coat the ingredients in the sauce and cook for an additional 1-2 minutes.
8. Serve the beef stir-fry with broccoli and bell peppers.

Nutritional values (per serving):

- Calories: 350
- Protein: 30g
- Fat: 15g
- Carbohydrates: 18g
- Fiber: 4g

Grilled Herb-Marinated Lamb Chops

Ingredients:

- 4 lamb chops
- 2 tablespoons of olive oil
- 2 cloves of garlic, minced
- 1 tablespoon of chopped fresh herbs (such as rosemary, thyme, or mint)
- Juice of 1 lemon
- Salt and pepper to taste

Directions:

1. In a bowl, whisk together the olive oil, minced garlic, chopped herbs, lemon juice, salt, and pepper to make the marinade.
2. Place the lamb chops in a shallow dish and pour the marinade over them, ensuring they are evenly coated.
3. Let the lamb chops marinate for at least 30 minutes or up to overnight in the refrigerator.
4. Preheat the grill to medium-high heat.
5. Remove the lamb chops from the marinade and discard the remaining marinade.
6. Grill the lamb chops for about 4-5 minutes per side for medium-rare doneness or adjust the cooking time to your preference.
7. Let the lamb chops rest for a few minutes before serving.

Nutritional values (per serving):

- Calories: 300
- Protein: 25g
- Fat: 20g
- Carbohydrates: 2g
- Fiber: 0g

Baked Chicken Thighs with Herbs and Garlic

Ingredients:

- 4 bone-in, skin-on chicken thighs
- 2 tablespoons of olive oil
- 4 cloves of garlic, minced
- 1 tablespoon of chopped fresh herbs (such as thyme, rosemary, or parsley)
- Salt and pepper to taste

Directions:

1. Preheat the oven to 400°F (200°C).
2. In a small bowl, mix together the olive oil, minced garlic, chopped herbs, salt, and pepper.
3. Place the chicken thighs in a baking dish and rub the herb and garlic mixture all over them, ensuring they are evenly coated.
4. Bake the chicken thighs in the preheated oven for about 30-35 minutes, or until the skin is crispy and the internal temperature reaches 165°F (74°C).
5. Let the chicken thighs rest for a few minutes before serving.

Nutritional values (per serving):

- Calories: 350
- Protein: 30g
- Fat: 25g
- Carbohydrates: 2g
- Fiber: 0g

Grilled Teriyaki Chicken Skewers

Ingredients:

- 1 pound of boneless, skinless chicken breasts, cut into cubes
- 1/4 cup of low-sodium soy sauce
- 2 tablespoons of honey
- 2 tablespoons of rice vinegar
- 1 tablespoon of sesame oil
- 2 cloves of garlic, minced
- 1 teaspoon of grated ginger
- Salt and pepper to taste
- Optional toppings: sesame seeds, sliced green onions

Directions:

1. In a bowl, whisk together the soy sauce, honey, rice vinegar, sesame oil, minced garlic, grated ginger, salt, and pepper to make the teriyaki marinade.
2. Place the chicken cubes in a shallow dish and pour the marinade over them, ensuring they are evenly coated. Let them marinate for at least 30 minutes in the refrigerator.
3. Preheat the grill to medium-high heat.
4. Thread the chicken cubes onto skewers.
5. Grill the chicken skewers for about 6-8 minutes per side, or until cooked through and the internal temperature reaches 165°F (74°C).

6. Brush the remaining marinade onto the chicken skewers while grilling.
7. Serve the teriyaki chicken skewers with a sprinkle of sesame seeds and sliced green onions, if desired.

Nutritional values (per serving):

- Calories: 250
- Protein: 30g
- Fat: 6g
- Carbohydrates: 16g
- Fiber: 0g

Beef and Broccoli Stir-Fry

Ingredients:

- 1 pound of beef sirloin, thinly sliced
- 2 cups of broccoli florets
- 1/2 cup of sliced mushrooms
- 1/4 cup of low-sodium soy sauce
- 2 tablespoons of oyster sauce
- 1 tablespoon of cornstarch
- 1 tablespoon of vegetable oil
- 2 cloves of garlic, minced
- Salt and pepper to taste
- Optional: sliced green onions for garnish

Directions:

1. In a small bowl, whisk together the soy sauce, oyster sauce, cornstarch, salt, and pepper to make the sauce.
2. In a large skillet or wok, heat the vegetable oil over high heat.

3. Add the minced garlic and stir-fry for about 30 seconds until fragrant.
4. Add the beef slices to the skillet and stir-fry for 2-3 minutes until browned. Remove from the skillet and set aside.
5. In the same skillet, add the broccoli florets and sliced mushrooms. Stir-fry for 3-4 minutes until the vegetables are crisp-tender.
6. Return the beef to the skillet and pour the sauce over the stir-fry.
7. Stir well to coat the ingredients in the sauce and cook for an additional 1-2 minutes.
8. Serve the beef and broccoli stir-fry with steamed rice or noodles.
9. Garnish with sliced green onions, if desired.

Nutritional values (per serving):

- Calories: 320
- Protein: 30g
- Fat: 12g
- Carbohydrates: 22g
- Fiber: 3g

Grilled Herb-Marinated Steak

Ingredients:

- 1 pound of steak (such as ribeye, sirloin, or strip steak)
- 2 tablespoons of olive oil
- 2 cloves of garlic, minced
- 1 tablespoon of chopped fresh herbs (such as rosemary, thyme, or parsley)
- Salt and pepper to taste

Directions:

1. In a bowl, whisk together the olive oil, minced garlic, chopped herbs, salt, and pepper to make the marinade.
2. Place the steak in a shallow dish and pour the marinade over it, ensuring it is evenly coated. Let it marinate for at least 30 minutes or up to overnight in the refrigerator.
3. Preheat the grill to medium-high heat.
4. Remove the steak from the marinade and discard the remaining marinade.
5. Grill the steak for about 4-6 minutes per side, or until cooked to your desired doneness.
6. Let the steak rest for a few minutes before slicing.

Nutritional values (per serving):

- Calories: 400
- Protein: 30g
- Fat: 30g
- Carbohydrates: 0g
- Fiber: 0g

Baked Herb-Crusted Chicken Breast

Ingredients:

- 2 boneless, skinless chicken breasts
- 2 tablespoons of olive oil
- 1 tablespoon of chopped fresh herbs (such as thyme, rosemary, or parsley)
- 2 cloves of garlic, minced
- Salt and pepper to taste

Directions:

1. Preheat the oven to 400°F (200°C).
2. In a small bowl, mix together the olive oil, chopped herbs, minced garlic, salt, and pepper.
3. Place the chicken breasts in a baking dish and rub the herb mixture all over them, ensuring they are evenly coated.
4. Bake the chicken breasts in the preheated oven for about 20-25 minutes, or until cooked through and no longer pink in the center.
5. Let the chicken breasts rest for a few minutes before serving.

Nutritional values (per serving):

- Calories: 250
- Protein: 30g
- Fat: 10g
- Carbohydrates: 0g
- Fiber: 0g

Pork Tenderloin with Mustard and Rosemary

Ingredients:

- 1 pound of pork tenderloin
- 2 tablespoons of Dijon mustard
- 1 tablespoon of fresh rosemary, chopped
- 2 cloves of garlic, minced
- 1 tablespoon of olive oil
- Salt and pepper to taste

Directions:

1. Preheat the oven to 375°F (190°C).

2. In a small bowl, mix together the Dijon mustard, chopped rosemary, minced garlic, salt, and pepper.
3. Rub the mustard mixture all over the pork tenderloin, ensuring it is evenly coated.
4. Heat the olive oil in an oven-safe skillet over medium-high heat.
5. Sear the pork tenderloin in the skillet for 2-3 minutes on each side until browned.
6. Transfer the skillet to the preheated oven and bake for about 20-25 minutes, or until the internal temperature reaches 145°F (63°C).
7. Remove the pork from the oven and let it rest for a few minutes before slicing.

Nutritional values (per serving):

- Calories: 280
- Protein: 35g
- Fat: 12g
- Carbohydrates: 2g
- Fiber: 0g

Grilled Honey Mustard Chicken

Ingredients:

- 4 boneless, skinless chicken breasts
- ¼ cup Dijon mustard
- ¼ cup honey
- 2 tablespoons olive oil
- 2 cloves garlic, minced
- Salt and pepper to taste
- Optional: Fresh parsley for garnish

Directions:

1. Preheat the grill to medium-high heat.
2. In a small bowl, whisk together the Dijon mustard, honey, olive oil, minced garlic, salt, and pepper to make the marinade.
3. Place the chicken breasts in a shallow dish and pour the marinade over them, ensuring they are evenly coated.
4. Let the chicken marinate for at least 30 minutes in the refrigerator.
5. Remove the chicken from the marinade and discard the remaining marinade.
6. Grill the chicken breasts for about 6-8 minutes per side, or until cooked through and the internal temperature reaches 165°F (74°C).
7. Let the chicken rest for a few minutes before serving.
8. Garnish with fresh parsley, if desired.

Nutritional values (per serving):

- Calories: 280
- Protein: 30g
- Fat: 10g
- Carbohydrates: 18g
- Fiber: 0g

Beef and Vegetable Stir-Fry

Ingredients:

- 1 pound beef sirloin, thinly sliced
- 2 tablespoons low-sodium soy sauce
- 2 tablespoons oyster sauce
- 1 tablespoon cornstarch
- 1 tablespoon vegetable oil
- 2 cloves garlic, minced
- 1 onion, thinly sliced

- 1 red bell pepper, thinly sliced
- 1 cup broccoli florets
- Salt and pepper to taste
- Optional: Sliced green onions for garnish

Directions:

1. In a small bowl, whisk together the soy sauce, oyster sauce, cornstarch, salt, and pepper to make the sauce.
2. In a large skillet or wok, heat the vegetable oil over high heat.
3. Add the minced garlic and stir-fry for about 30 seconds until fragrant.
4. Add the beef slices to the skillet and stir-fry for 2-3 minutes until browned. Remove from the skillet and set aside.
5. In the same skillet, add the sliced onion, red bell pepper, and broccoli florets. Stir-fry for 3-4 minutes until the vegetables are crisp-tender.
6. Return the beef to the skillet and pour the sauce over the stir-fry.
7. Stir well to coat the ingredients in the sauce and cook for an additional 1-2 minutes.
8. Serve the beef and vegetable stir-fry hot.
9. Garnish with sliced green onions, if desired.

Nutritional values (per serving):

- Calories: 320
- Protein: 28g
- Fat: 12g
- Carbohydrates: 22g
- Fiber: 4g

Grilled Garlic and Herb Steak

Ingredients:

- 1 pound of steak (such as ribeye, sirloin, or strip steak)
- 4 cloves of garlic, minced
- 2 tablespoons of chopped fresh herbs (such as rosemary, thyme, or parsley)
- 2 tablespoons of olive oil
- Salt and pepper to taste

Directions:

1. In a small bowl, mix together the minced garlic, chopped herbs, olive oil, salt, and pepper to make a marinade.
2. Place the steak in a shallow dish and pour the marinade over it, ensuring it is evenly coated. Let it marinate for at least 30 minutes in the refrigerator.
3. Preheat the grill to medium-high heat.
4. Remove the steak from the marinade and discard the remaining marinade.
5. Grill the steak for about 4-6 minutes per side, or until cooked to your desired doneness.
6. Let the steak rest for a few minutes before slicing.

Nutritional values (per serving):

- Calories: 400
- Protein: 30g
- Fat: 30g
- Carbohydrates: 0g
- Fiber: 0g

Baked Herb-Crusted Chicken Thighs

Ingredients:

- 4 bone-in, skin-on chicken thighs
- 2 tablespoons of olive oil
- 1 tablespoon of chopped fresh herbs (such as thyme, rosemary, or parsley)
- 2 cloves of garlic, minced
- Salt and pepper to taste

Directions:

1. Preheat the oven to 400°F (200°C).
2. In a small bowl, mix together the olive oil, chopped herbs, minced garlic, salt, and pepper.
3. Place the chicken thighs in a baking dish and rub the herb mixture all over them, ensuring they are evenly coated.
4. Bake the chicken thighs in the preheated oven for about 30-35 minutes, or until cooked through and the internal temperature reaches 165°F (74°C).
5. Let the chicken thighs rest for a few minutes before serving.

Nutritional values (per serving):

- Calories: 350
- Protein: 30g
- Fat: 20g
- Carbohydrates: 0g
- Fiber: 0g

Pork Tenderloin with Mustard and Herb Crust

Ingredients:

- 1 pound of pork tenderloin
- 2 tablespoons of Dijon mustard
- 1 tablespoon of chopped fresh herbs (such as thyme, rosemary, or sage)
- 2 cloves of garlic, minced
- 1 tablespoon of olive oil
- Salt and pepper to taste

Directions:

1. Preheat the oven to 375°F (190°C).
2. In a small bowl, mix together the Dijon mustard, chopped herbs, minced garlic, salt, and pepper.
3. Rub the mustard and herb mixture all over the pork tenderloin, ensuring it is evenly coated.
4. Heat the olive oil in an oven-safe skillet over medium-high heat.
5. Sear the pork tenderloin in the skillet for 2-3 minutes on each side until browned.
6. Transfer the skillet to the preheated oven and bake for about 20-25 minutes, or until the internal temperature reaches 145°F (63°C).
7. Remove the pork from the oven and let it rest for a few minutes before slicing.

Nutritional values (per serving):

- Calories: 280
- Protein: 35g
- Fat: 12g
- Carbohydrates: 2g
- Fiber: 0g

Grilled Lemon Garlic Chicken

Ingredients:

- 4 boneless, skinless chicken breasts
- Juice of 2 lemons
- 4 cloves of garlic, minced
- 2 tablespoons of olive oil
- Salt and pepper to taste
- Optional: Fresh parsley for garnish

Directions:

1. Preheat the grill to medium-high heat.
2. In a small bowl, whisk together the lemon juice, minced garlic, olive oil, salt, and pepper to make the marinade.
3. Place the chicken breasts in a shallow dish and pour the marinade over them, ensuring they are evenly coated. Let them marinate for at least 30 minutes in the refrigerator.
4. Remove the chicken from the marinade and discard the remaining marinade.
5. Grill the chicken breasts for about 6-8 minutes per side, or until cooked through and the internal temperature reaches 165°F (74°C).
6. Let the chicken rest for a few minutes before serving.
7. Garnish with fresh parsley, if desired.

Nutritional values (per serving):

- Calories: 300
- Protein: 30g
- Fat: 10g
- Carbohydrates: 4g
- Fiber: 0g

Beef and Broccoli Skillet

Ingredients:

- 1 pound of beef sirloin, thinly sliced
- 2 cups of broccoli florets
- 1 onion, thinly sliced
- 2 cloves of garlic, minced
- 2 tablespoons of low-sodium soy sauce
- 1 tablespoon of oyster sauce
- 1 tablespoon of cornstarch
- 1 tablespoon of vegetable oil
- Salt and pepper to taste

Directions:

1. In a small bowl, whisk together the soy sauce, oyster sauce, cornstarch, salt, and pepper to make the sauce.
2. In a large skillet, heat the vegetable oil over medium-high heat.
3. Add the minced garlic and sliced onion to the skillet and sauté until fragrant and slightly softened.
4. Add the beef slices to the skillet and stir-fry for 2-3 minutes until browned.
5. Add the broccoli florets to the skillet and continue to stir-fry for an additional 2-3 minutes until the broccoli is crisp-tender.
6. Pour the sauce over the beef and broccoli in the skillet and stir well to coat.
7. Cook for another 1-2 minutes until the sauce thickens and everything is well combined.
8. Serve hot.

Nutritional values (per serving):

- Calories: 350
- Protein: 30g
- Fat: 15g

- Carbohydrates: 14g
- Fiber: 3g

---◆---

Grilled Herb-Marinated Chicken Breast

Ingredients:

- 4 boneless, skinless chicken breasts
- 2 tablespoons of olive oil
- 2 cloves of garlic, minced
- 1 tablespoon of chopped fresh herbs (such as rosemary, thyme, or basil)
- Juice of 1 lemon
- Salt and pepper to taste

Directions:

1. In a bowl, whisk together the olive oil, minced garlic, chopped herbs, lemon juice, salt, and pepper to make the marinade.
2. Place the chicken breasts in a shallow dish and pour the marinade over them, ensuring they are evenly coated.
3. Let the chicken breasts marinate for at least 30 minutes or up to overnight in the refrigerator.
4. Preheat the grill to medium-high heat.
5. Remove the chicken breasts from the marinade and discard the remaining marinade.
6. Grill the chicken breasts for about 6-8 minutes per side, or until cooked through and the internal temperature reaches 165°F (74°C).
7. Let the chicken breasts rest for a few minutes before serving.

Nutritional values (per serving):

- Calories: 250
- Protein: 30g
- Fat: 10g
- Carbohydrates: 2g
- Fiber: 0g

Beef Stir-Fry with Vegetables

Ingredients:

- 1 pound of beef sirloin, thinly sliced
- 2 cups of mixed vegetables (such as bell peppers, broccoli, and carrots)
- 2 tablespoons of low-sodium soy sauce
- 1 tablespoon of oyster sauce
- 1 tablespoon of cornstarch
- 1 tablespoon of vegetable oil
- 2 cloves of garlic, minced
- Salt and pepper to taste

Directions:

1. In a small bowl, whisk together the soy sauce, oyster sauce, cornstarch, salt, and pepper to make the sauce.
2. In a large skillet or wok, heat the vegetable oil over high heat.
3. Add the minced garlic and stir-fry for about 30 seconds until fragrant.
4. Add the beef slices to the skillet and stir-fry for 2-3 minutes until browned. Remove from the skillet and set aside.
5. In the same skillet, add the mixed vegetables and stir-fry for 3-4 minutes until they are crisp-tender.
6. Return the beef to the skillet and pour the sauce over the stir-fry.

7. Stir well to coat the ingredients in the sauce and cook for an additional 1-2 minutes.
8. Serve the beef stir-fry hot.

Nutritional values (per serving):

- Calories: 300
- Protein: 25g
- Fat: 12g
- Carbohydrates: 20g
- Fiber: 4g

Grilled Lemon Herb Chicken

Ingredients:

- 4 boneless, skinless chicken breasts
- Juice of 2 lemons
- Zest of 1 lemon
- 2 tablespoons of olive oil
- 2 cloves of garlic, minced
- 1 tablespoon of chopped fresh herbs (such as rosemary, thyme, or parsley)
- Salt and pepper to taste

Directions:

1. In a bowl, whisk together the lemon juice, lemon zest, olive oil, minced garlic, chopped herbs, salt, and pepper to make the marinade.
2. Place the chicken breasts in a shallow dish and pour the marinade over them, ensuring they are evenly coated.
3. Let the chicken breasts marinate for at least 30 minutes in the refrigerator.
4. Preheat the grill to medium-high heat.

5. Remove the chicken breasts from the marinade and discard the remaining marinade.
6. Grill the chicken breasts for about 6-8 minutes per side, or until cooked through and the internal temperature reaches 165°F (74°C).
7. Let the chicken breasts rest for a few minutes before serving.

Nutritional values (per serving):

- Calories: 250
- Protein: 30g
- Fat: 10g
- Carbohydrates: 2g
- Fiber: 0g

Beef and Vegetable Stir-Fry

Ingredients:

- 1 pound of beef sirloin, thinly sliced
- 2 cups of mixed vegetables (such as bell peppers, broccoli, and carrots)
- 2 tablespoons of low-sodium soy sauce
- 1 tablespoon of oyster sauce
- 1 tablespoon of cornstarch
- 1 tablespoon of vegetable oil
- 2 cloves of garlic, minced
- Salt and pepper to taste

Directions:

1. In a small bowl, whisk together the soy sauce, oyster sauce, cornstarch, salt, and pepper to make the sauce.

2. In a large skillet or wok, heat the vegetable oil over high heat.
3. Add the minced garlic and stir-fry for about 30 seconds until fragrant.
4. Add the beef slices to the skillet and stir-fry for 2-3 minutes until browned. Remove from the skillet and set aside.
5. In the same skillet, add the mixed vegetables and stir-fry for 3-4 minutes until they are crisp-tender.
6. Return the beef to the skillet and pour the sauce over the stir-fry.
7. Stir well to coat the ingredients in the sauce and cook for an additional 1-2 minutes.
8. Serve the beef stir-fry hot.

Nutritional values (per serving):

- Calories: 300
- Protein: 25g
- Fat: 12g
- Carbohydrates: 20g
- Fiber: 4g

Grilled Chimichurri Steak

Ingredients:

- 1 pound of steak (such as ribeye, sirloin, or flank steak)
- 1 cup of fresh parsley leaves
- 3 cloves of garlic
- 2 tablespoons of red wine vinegar
- 2 tablespoons of olive oil
- 1 teaspoon of dried oregano
- Salt and pepper to taste

Directions:

1. In a blender or food processor, combine the parsley, garlic, red wine vinegar, olive oil, dried oregano, salt, and pepper. Blend until smooth to make the chimichurri sauce.
2. Place the steak in a shallow dish and pour half of the chimichurri sauce over it, reserving the rest for serving. Ensure the steak is evenly coated and let it marinate for at least 30 minutes in the refrigerator.
3. Preheat the grill to medium-high heat.
4. Remove the steak from the marinade and discard the remaining marinade.
5. Grill the steak for about 4-6 minutes per side, or until cooked to your desired doneness.
6. Let the steak rest for a few minutes before slicing. Serve with the reserved chimichurri sauce on the side.

Nutritional values (per serving):

*   Calories: 400
*   Protein: 30g
*   Fat: 30g
*   Carbohydrates: 2g
*   Fiber: 1g

Baked Italian Herb Chicken Thighs

Ingredients:

*   4 bone-in, skin-on chicken thighs
*   2 tablespoons of olive oil
*   2 teaspoons of dried Italian herb seasoning
*   1 teaspoon of garlic powder
*   1 teaspoon of onion powder
*   Salt and pepper to taste

Directions:

1. Preheat the oven to 400°F (200°C).
2. In a small bowl, mix together the olive oil, Italian herb seasoning, garlic powder, onion powder, salt, and pepper.
3. Place the chicken thighs in a baking dish and rub the herb mixture all over them, ensuring they are evenly coated.
4. Bake the chicken thighs in the preheated oven for about 30-35 minutes, or until cooked through and the internal temperature reaches 165°F (74°C).
5. Let the chicken thighs rest for a few minutes before serving.

Nutritional values (per serving):

- Calories: 350
- Protein: 25g
- Fat: 25g
- Carbohydrates: 1g
- Fiber: 0g

Grilled Cajun Chicken

Ingredients:

- 4 boneless, skinless chicken breasts
- 2 teaspoons of paprika
- 1 teaspoon of garlic powder
- 1 teaspoon of onion powder
- 1 teaspoon of dried oregano
- 1 teaspoon of dried thyme
- 1/2 teaspoon of cayenne pepper
- Salt and pepper to taste
- Olive oil for brushing

Directions:

1. Preheat the grill to medium-high heat.
2. In a small bowl, mix together the paprika, garlic powder, onion powder, dried oregano, dried thyme, cayenne pepper, salt, and pepper to make the Cajun spice rub.
3. Brush the chicken breasts with olive oil on both sides.
4. Sprinkle the Cajun spice rub over the chicken breasts, ensuring they are evenly coated.
5. Grill the chicken breasts for about 6-8 minutes per side, or until cooked through and the internal temperature reaches 165°F (74°C).
6. Let the chicken rest for a few minutes before serving.

Nutritional values (per serving):

- Calories: 250
- Protein: 30g
- Fat: 8g
- Carbohydrates: 2g
- Fiber: 1g

Beef and Vegetable Kabobs

Ingredients:

- 1 pound of beef sirloin, cut into cubes
- 1 red bell pepper, cut into chunks
- 1 green bell pepper, cut into chunks
- 1 red onion, cut into chunks
- 8-10 cherry tomatoes
- 2 tablespoons of olive oil
- 2 cloves of garlic, minced
- 1 teaspoon of dried oregano
- 1 teaspoon of dried thyme

- Salt and pepper to taste
- Skewers

Directions:

1. In a bowl, whisk together the olive oil, minced garlic, dried oregano, dried thyme, salt, and pepper to make the marinade.
2. Thread the beef cubes, bell peppers, onion chunks, and cherry tomatoes onto skewers.
3. Place the kabobs in a shallow dish and brush the marinade over them, ensuring they are evenly coated. Let them marinate for at least 30 minutes in the refrigerator.
4. Preheat the grill to medium-high heat.
5. Grill the kabobs for about 10-12 minutes, turning occasionally, until the beef is cooked to your desired doneness.
6. Remove the kabobs from the grill and let them rest for a few minutes before serving.

Nutritional values (per serving):

- Calories: 300
- Protein: 25g
- Fat: 12g
- Carbohydrates: 10g
- Fiber: 3g

FISH & SEAFOOD

Grilled Lemon Garlic Salmon

Ingredients:

- 4 salmon fillets
- Juice of 2 lemons
- 4 cloves of garlic, minced
- 2 tablespoons of olive oil
- Salt and pepper to taste
- Optional: Fresh dill for garnish

Directions:

1. Preheat the grill to medium-high heat.
2. In a small bowl, whisk together the lemon juice, minced garlic, olive oil, salt, and pepper to make the marinade.
3. Place the salmon fillets in a shallow dish and pour the marinade over them, ensuring they are evenly coated.
4. Let the salmon marinate for at least 30 minutes in the refrigerator.
5. Remove the salmon from the marinade and discard the remaining marinade.
6. Grill the salmon fillets for about 4-6 minutes per side, or until cooked through and flaky.
7. Garnish with fresh dill, if desired.

Nutritional values (per serving):

- Calories: 350
- Protein: 30g
- Fat: 20g
- Carbohydrates: 2g
- Fiber: 0g

Shrimp Stir-Fry with Vegetables

Ingredients:

- 1 pound of shrimp, peeled and deveined
- 2 cups of mixed vegetables (such as bell peppers, broccoli, and snap peas)
- 2 cloves of garlic, minced
- 2 tablespoons of low-sodium soy sauce
- 1 tablespoon of oyster sauce
- 1 tablespoon of cornstarch
- 1 tablespoon of vegetable oil
- Salt and pepper to taste

Directions:

1. In a small bowl, whisk together the soy sauce, oyster sauce, cornstarch, salt, and pepper to make the sauce.
2. In a large skillet or wok, heat the vegetable oil over high heat.
3. Add the minced garlic and stir-fry for about 30 seconds until fragrant.
4. Add the shrimp to the skillet and stir-fry for 2-3 minutes until pink and cooked through. Remove from the skillet and set aside.
5. In the same skillet, add the mixed vegetables and stir-fry for 3-4 minutes until they are crisp-tender.
6. Return the shrimp to the skillet and pour the sauce over the stir-fry.
7. Stir well to coat the ingredients in the sauce and cook for an additional 1-2 minutes.
8. Serve the shrimp stir-fry hot.

Nutritional values (per serving):

- Calories: 250
- Protein: 25g
- Fat: 8g

- Carbohydrates: 12g
- Fiber: 3g

❖

Baked Lemon Herb Cod

Ingredients:

- 4 cod fillets
- Juice of 2 lemons
- Zest of 1 lemon
- 2 tablespoons of olive oil
- 2 cloves of garlic, minced
- 1 tablespoon of chopped fresh herbs (such as parsley, dill, or basil)
- Salt and pepper to taste

Directions:

1. Preheat the oven to 375°F (190°C).
2. In a small bowl, whisk together the lemon juice, lemon zest, olive oil, minced garlic, chopped herbs, salt, and pepper.
3. Place the cod fillets in a baking dish and pour the marinade over them, ensuring they are evenly coated.
4. Let the cod fillets marinate for about 15-20 minutes.
5. Bake the cod fillets in the preheated oven for about 15-20 minutes, or until cooked through and flaky.
6. Serve the baked cod hot.

Nutritional values (per serving):

- Calories: 200
- Protein: 30g
- Fat: 8g
- Carbohydrates: 2g

- Fiber: 0g

◆

Grilled Shrimp Skewers

Ingredients:

- 1 pound of shrimp, peeled and deveined
- 2 tablespoons of olive oil
- 2 cloves of garlic, minced
- 1 tablespoon of lemon juice
- 1 teaspoon of paprika
- Salt and pepper to taste
- Skewers

Directions:

1. Preheat the grill to medium-high heat.
2. In a bowl, combine the olive oil, minced garlic, lemon juice, paprika, salt, and pepper to make the marinade.
3. Thread the shrimp onto skewers, leaving a little space between each shrimp.
4. Brush the shrimp skewers with the marinade, ensuring they are evenly coated.
5. Grill the shrimp skewers for about 2-3 minutes per side, or until the shrimp is pink and cooked through.
6. Serve the grilled shrimp skewers hot.

Nutritional values (per serving):

- Calories: 150
- Protein: 20g
- Fat: 7g
- Carbohydrates: 1g
- Fiber: 0g

Pan-Seared Sesame Tuna Steaks

Ingredients:

- 4 tuna steaks
- 2 tablespoons of soy sauce
- 1 tablespoon of sesame oil
- 1 tablespoon of sesame seeds
- 1 teaspoon of grated ginger
- Salt and pepper to taste
- 1 tablespoon of vegetable oil for cooking

Directions:

1. In a shallow dish, whisk together the soy sauce, sesame oil, sesame seeds, grated ginger, salt, and pepper to make the marinade.
2. Place the tuna steaks in the marinade and let them marinate for about 15-20 minutes.
3. Heat the vegetable oil in a skillet over high heat.
4. Remove the tuna steaks from the marinade and discard the remaining marinade.
5. Sear the tuna steaks in the hot skillet for about 1-2 minutes per side, or until the desired doneness.
6. Remove the tuna steaks from the skillet and let them rest for a few minutes before serving.

Nutritional values (per serving):

- Calories: 250
- Protein: 30g
- Fat: 12g
- Carbohydrates: 2g
- Fiber: 0g

Grilled Lemon Garlic Shrimp Skewers

Ingredients:

- 1 pound of large shrimp, peeled and deveined
- Juice of 2 lemons
- 4 cloves of garlic, minced
- 2 tablespoons of olive oil
- Salt and pepper to taste
- Wooden or metal skewers

Directions:

1. Preheat the grill to medium-high heat.
2. In a small bowl, whisk together the lemon juice, minced garlic, olive oil, salt, and pepper to make the marinade.
3. Thread the shrimp onto skewers, leaving a little space between each shrimp.
4. Place the shrimp skewers in a shallow dish and pour the marinade over them, ensuring they are evenly coated. Let them marinate for about 15 minutes.
5. Remove the shrimp skewers from the marinade and discard the remaining marinade.
6. Grill the shrimp skewers for about 2-3 minutes per side, or until the shrimp is pink and cooked through.
7. Serve the grilled shrimp skewers hot.

Nutritional values (per serving):

- Calories: 200
- Protein: 25g
- Fat: 8g
- Carbohydrates: 4g
- Fiber: 0g

Pan-Seared Scallops with Garlic Butter Sauce

Ingredients:

- 1 pound of scallops
- 2 tablespoons of butter
- 2 cloves of garlic, minced
- Juice of 1 lemon
- Salt and pepper to taste
- Chopped parsley for garnish

Directions:

1. Pat the scallops dry with a paper towel and season them with salt and pepper.
2. In a large skillet, melt the butter over medium-high heat.
3. Add the minced garlic to the skillet and cook for about 1 minute until fragrant.
4. Place the scallops in the skillet and sear them for about 2-3 minutes per side until golden brown and cooked through.
5. Drizzle the lemon juice over the scallops and toss them gently in the garlic butter sauce.
6. Transfer the scallops to a serving plate and garnish with chopped parsley.
7. Serve the pan-seared scallops hot.

Nutritional values (per serving):

- Calories: 250
- Protein: 20g
- Fat: 14g
- Carbohydrates: 6g
- Fiber: 0g

Baked Cod with Tomato Basil Salsa

Ingredients:

- 4 cod fillets
- 2 cups of diced tomatoes
- 1/4 cup of chopped fresh basil
- 2 tablespoons of olive oil
- 2 cloves of garlic, minced
- Juice of 1 lemon
- Salt and pepper to taste

Directions:

1. Preheat the oven to 375°F (190°C).
2. In a bowl, combine the diced tomatoes, chopped basil, minced garlic, olive oil, lemon juice, salt, and pepper to make the salsa.
3. Place the cod fillets in a baking dish and spoon the tomato basil salsa over them, ensuring they are evenly coated.
4. Bake the cod fillets in the preheated oven for about 15-20 minutes, or until cooked through and flaky.
5. Serve the baked cod with the tomato basil salsa on top.

Nutritional values (per serving):

- Calories: 200
- Protein: 30g
- Fat: 8g
- Carbohydrates: 6g
- Fiber: 2g

Grilled Teriyaki Salmon

Ingredients:

- 4 salmon fillets
- 1/4 cup of low-sodium soy sauce
- 2 tablespoons of honey
- 2 tablespoons of rice vinegar
- 1 tablespoon of grated ginger
- 2 cloves of garlic, minced
- 1 tablespoon of sesame oil
- Optional: Sesame seeds and green onions for garnish

Directions:

1. Preheat the grill to medium-high heat.
2. In a small bowl, whisk together the soy sauce, honey, rice vinegar, grated ginger, minced garlic, and sesame oil to make the teriyaki marinade.
3. Place the salmon fillets in a shallow dish and pour the teriyaki marinade over them, ensuring they are evenly coated. Let them marinate for at least 30 minutes in the refrigerator.
4. Remove the salmon from the marinade and discard the remaining marinade.
5. Grill the salmon fillets for about 4-6 minutes per side, or until cooked through and flaky.
6. Garnish with sesame seeds and green onions, if desired.

Nutritional values (per serving):

- Calories: 300
- Protein: 30g
- Fat: 15g
- Carbohydrates: 10g
- Fiber: 0g

Spicy Garlic Shrimp Stir-Fry

Ingredients:

- 1 pound of shrimp, peeled and deveined
- 2 tablespoons of olive oil
- 4 cloves of garlic, minced
- 1 red bell pepper, sliced
- 1 yellow bell pepper, sliced
- 1 medium zucchini, sliced
- 1 tablespoon of low-sodium soy sauce
- 1 tablespoon of sriracha sauce (adjust to taste)
- Salt and pepper to taste
- Chopped cilantro for garnish

Directions:

1. In a large skillet or wok, heat the olive oil over medium-high heat.
2. Add the minced garlic and stir-fry for about 30 seconds until fragrant.
3. Add the shrimp to the skillet and cook for 2-3 minutes until pink and cooked through. Remove the shrimp from the skillet and set aside.
4. In the same skillet, add the sliced bell peppers and zucchini. Stir-fry for 3-4 minutes until crisp-tender.
5. Return the shrimp to the skillet and add the soy sauce and sriracha sauce. Stir well to coat the ingredients and cook for an additional 1-2 minutes.
6. Season with salt and pepper to taste.
7. Garnish with chopped cilantro before serving.

Nutritional values (per serving):

- Calories: 250
- Protein: 25g
- Fat: 10g
- Carbohydrates: 10g

- Fiber: 3g

---◆---

Grilled Cajun Shrimp Skewers

Ingredients:

- 1 pound of shrimp, peeled and deveined
- 2 tablespoons of olive oil
- 2 teaspoons of Cajun seasoning
- Juice of 1 lemon
- Salt and pepper to taste
- Skewers

Directions:

1. Preheat the grill to medium-high heat.
2. In a bowl, combine the olive oil, Cajun seasoning, lemon juice, salt, and pepper to make the marinade.
3. Thread the shrimp onto skewers, leaving a little space between each shrimp.
4. Brush the shrimp skewers with the marinade, ensuring they are evenly coated.
5. Grill the shrimp skewers for about 2-3 minutes per side, or until the shrimp is pink and cooked through.
6. Serve the grilled Cajun shrimp skewers hot.

Nutritional values (per serving):

- Calories: 150
- Protein: 25g
- Fat: 5g
- Carbohydrates: 2g
- Fiber: 0g

Baked Lemon Herb Halibut

Ingredients:

- 4 halibut fillets
- Juice of 1 lemon
- 2 tablespoons of olive oil
- 2 cloves of garlic, minced
- 1 tablespoon of chopped fresh herbs (such as parsley, dill, or basil)
- Salt and pepper to taste

Directions:

1. Preheat the oven to 375°F (190°C).
2. In a small bowl, whisk together the lemon juice, olive oil, minced garlic, chopped herbs, salt, and pepper.
3. Place the halibut fillets in a baking dish and pour the marinade over them, ensuring they are evenly coated.
4. Bake the halibut fillets in the preheated oven for about 15-20 minutes, or until cooked through and flaky.
5. Serve the baked lemon herb halibut hot.

Nutritional values (per serving):

- Calories: 200
- Protein: 30g
- Fat: 8g
- Carbohydrates: 2g
- Fiber: 0g

Grilled Tuna Steaks with Mango Salsa

Ingredients:

- 4 tuna steaks
- 2 tablespoons of olive oil
- Juice of 1 lime
- 1 teaspoon of ground cumin
- Salt and pepper to taste

Mango Salsa:

- 1 ripe mango, peeled and diced
- 1/2 red bell pepper, diced
- 1/4 red onion, finely chopped
- Juice of 1 lime
- 2 tablespoons of chopped fresh cilantro
- Salt to taste

Directions:

1. Preheat the grill to medium-high heat.
2. In a small bowl, whisk together the olive oil, lime juice, ground cumin, salt, and pepper to make the marinade.
3. Brush the tuna steaks with the marinade, ensuring they are evenly coated.
4. Grill the tuna steaks for about 2-3 minutes per side for medium-rare, or adjust the cooking time to your desired doneness.
5. In a separate bowl, combine all the ingredients for the mango salsa and mix well.
6. Serve the grilled tuna steaks hot, topped with the mango salsa.

Nutritional values (per serving):

- Calories: 250
- Protein: 30g

- Fat: 10g
- Carbohydrates: 10g
- Fiber: 2g

Grilled Lime-Cilantro Mahi Mahi

Ingredients:

- 4 mahi mahi fillets
- Juice of 2 limes
- Zest of 1 lime
- 2 tablespoons of chopped fresh cilantro
- 2 cloves of garlic, minced
- 2 tablespoons of olive oil
- Salt and pepper to taste

Directions:

1. Preheat the grill to medium-high heat.
2. In a small bowl, whisk together the lime juice, lime zest, chopped cilantro, minced garlic, olive oil, salt, and pepper to make the marinade.
3. Place the mahi mahi fillets in a shallow dish and pour the marinade over them, ensuring they are evenly coated. Let them marinate for at least 30 minutes in the refrigerator.
4. Remove the mahi mahi fillets from the marinade and discard the remaining marinade.
5. Grill the mahi mahi fillets for about 4-6 minutes per side, or until cooked through and flaky.
6. Serve the grilled lime-cilantro mahi mahi hot.

Nutritional values (per serving):

- Calories: 200
- Protein: 30g

- Fat: 8g
- Carbohydrates: 2g
- Fiber: 0g

Baked Coconut Shrimp

Ingredients:

- 1 pound of shrimp, peeled and deveined
- 1 cup of shredded unsweetened coconut
- 1/2 cup of panko breadcrumbs
- 2 eggs, beaten
- Salt and pepper to taste
- Optional: Sweet chili sauce for dipping

Directions:

1. Preheat the oven to 425°F (220°C). Line a baking sheet with parchment paper.
2. In a shallow dish, combine the shredded coconut and panko breadcrumbs.
3. Season the shrimp with salt and pepper.
4. Dip each shrimp into the beaten eggs, allowing any excess to drip off, then coat it with the coconut breadcrumb mixture. Press gently to adhere the coating.
5. Place the coated shrimp on the prepared baking sheet and repeat with the remaining shrimp.
6. Bake the coconut shrimp in the preheated oven for about 12-15 minutes, or until golden brown and crispy.
7. Serve the baked coconut shrimp hot, with sweet chili sauce for dipping if desired.

Nutritional values (per serving):

- Calories: 250

- Protein: 20g
- Fat: 15g
- Carbohydrates: 10g
- Fiber: 2g

Seared Scallops with Lemon Butter Sauce

Ingredients:

- 1 pound of scallops
- 2 tablespoons of butter
- 2 cloves of garlic, minced
- Juice of 1 lemon
- Salt and pepper to taste
- Chopped parsley for garnish

Directions:

1. Pat the scallops dry with a paper towel and season them with salt and pepper.
2. In a large skillet, melt the butter over medium-high heat.
3. Add the minced garlic to the skillet and cook for about 1 minute until fragrant.
4. Place the scallops in the skillet and sear them for about 2-3 minutes per side until golden brown and cooked through.
5. Drizzle the lemon juice over the scallops and toss them gently in the garlic butter sauce.
6. Transfer the scallops to a serving plate and garnish with chopped parsley.
7. Serve the seared scallops with lemon butter sauce hot.

Nutritional values (per serving):

- Calories: 200
- Protein: 25g
- Fat: 10g
- Carbohydrates: 2g

Grilled Garlic Butter Salmon

Ingredients:

- 4 salmon fillets
- 4 tablespoons of butter, melted
- 4 cloves of garlic, minced
- Juice of 1 lemon
- Salt and pepper to taste
- Optional: Fresh dill for garnish

Directions:

1. Preheat the grill to medium-high heat.
2. In a small bowl, combine the melted butter, minced garlic, lemon juice, salt, and pepper to make the garlic butter sauce.
3. Place the salmon fillets on a piece of aluminum foil and brush them with the garlic butter sauce, ensuring they are evenly coated.
4. Grill the salmon fillets on the foil for about 6-8 minutes per side, or until cooked through and flaky.
5. Remove the salmon from the grill and garnish with fresh dill, if desired.

Nutritional values (per serving):

- Calories: 350
- Protein: 30g
- Fat: 22g

- Carbohydrates: 2g
- Fiber: 0g

Lemon Herb Grilled Shrimp

Ingredients:

- 1 pound of shrimp, peeled and deveined
- Juice of 2 lemons
- Zest of 1 lemon
- 2 tablespoons of olive oil
- 2 cloves of garlic, minced
- 1 tablespoon of chopped fresh herbs (such as parsley, basil, or thyme)
- Salt and pepper to taste

Directions:

1. Preheat the grill to medium-high heat.
2. In a small bowl, whisk together the lemon juice, lemon zest, olive oil, minced garlic, chopped herbs, salt, and pepper to make the marinade.
3. Place the shrimp in a shallow dish and pour the marinade over them, ensuring they are evenly coated. Let them marinate for about 15 minutes.
4. Thread the shrimp onto skewers, leaving a little space between each shrimp.
5. Grill the shrimp skewers for about 2-3 minutes per side, or until the shrimp is pink and cooked through.
6. Serve the grilled lemon herb shrimp hot.

Nutritional values (per serving):

- Calories: 200
- Protein: 25g

- Fat: 8g
- Carbohydrates: 2g
- Fiber: 0g

Baked Cod with Mediterranean Salsa

Ingredients:

- 4 cod fillets
- 2 cups of diced tomatoes
- 1/4 cup of sliced black olives
- 1/4 cup of chopped fresh basil
- 2 tablespoons of olive oil
- 2 cloves of garlic, minced
- Juice of 1 lemon
- Salt and pepper to taste

Directions:

1. Preheat the oven to 375°F (190°C).
2. In a bowl, combine the diced tomatoes, black olives, chopped basil, minced garlic, olive oil, lemon juice, salt, and pepper to make the Mediterranean salsa.
3. Place the cod fillets in a baking dish and spoon the Mediterranean salsa over them, ensuring they are evenly coated.
4. Bake the cod fillets in the preheated oven for about 15-20 minutes, or until cooked through and flaky.
5. Serve the baked cod with the Mediterranean salsa on top.

Nutritional values (per serving):

- Calories: 200

- Protein: 30g
- Fat: 8g
- Carbohydrates: 6g
- Fiber: 2g

DESSERTS

Chocolate Protein Mug Cake

Ingredients:

- 1 scoop of chocolate protein powder
- 2 tablespoons of almond flour
- 1 tablespoon of unsweetened cocoa powder
- 1/4 teaspoon of baking powder
- 1 tablespoon of almond butter
- 1/4 cup of unsweetened almond milk
- 1/2 teaspoon of vanilla extract
- Optional: Sugar-free chocolate chips for topping

Directions:

1. In a microwave-safe mug, combine the chocolate protein powder, almond flour, cocoa powder, and baking powder.
2. Add the almond butter, almond milk, and vanilla extract to the mug. Stir well until the ingredients are fully combined.
3. Microwave the mug on high for about 1-2 minutes, or until the cake is set and cooked through.
4. Remove the mug from the microwave and let it cool for a few minutes.
5. Optional: Sprinkle sugar-free chocolate chips on top of the mug cake.
6. Enjoy the chocolate protein mug cake warm.

Nutritional values (per serving):

- Calories: 250
- Protein: 30g
- Fat: 10g
- Carbohydrates: 10g
- Fiber: 4g

Vanilla Protein Pancakes

Ingredients:

- 1 scoop of vanilla protein powder
- 1/4 cup of almond flour
- 1/4 teaspoon of baking powder
- 1/4 teaspoon of cinnamon
- 2 egg whites
- 1/4 cup of unsweetened almond milk
- 1/2 teaspoon of vanilla extract

Directions:

1. In a bowl, whisk together the vanilla protein powder, almond flour, baking powder, and cinnamon.
2. In a separate bowl, whisk the egg whites, almond milk, and vanilla extract until well combined.
3. Add the wet ingredients to the dry ingredients and stir until a smooth batter forms.
4. Heat a non-stick skillet or griddle over medium heat and lightly coat it with cooking spray.
5. Pour about 1/4 cup of the batter onto the skillet to form each pancake.
6. Cook the pancakes for about 2-3 minutes on each side, or until golden brown and cooked through.
7. Serve the vanilla protein pancakes warm with your favorite toppings, such as fresh berries or sugar-free syrup.

Nutritional values (per serving):

- Calories: 200
- Protein: 25g
- Fat: 8g
- Carbohydrates: 8g
- Fiber: 2g

Chocolate Protein Mug Brownie

Ingredients:

- 1 scoop of chocolate protein powder
- 2 tablespoons of almond flour
- 1 tablespoon of unsweetened cocoa powder
- 1/4 teaspoon of baking powder
- 1 tablespoon of almond butter
- 1/4 cup of unsweetened almond milk
- 1/2 teaspoon of vanilla extract
- Optional: Sugar-free chocolate chips for topping

Directions:

1. In a microwave-safe mug, combine the chocolate protein powder, almond flour, cocoa powder, and baking powder.
2. Add the almond butter, almond milk, and vanilla extract to the mug. Stir well until the ingredients are fully combined.
3. Microwave the mug on high for about 1-2 minutes, or until the brownie is set and cooked through.
4. Remove the mug from the microwave and let it cool for a few minutes.
5. Optional: Sprinkle sugar-free chocolate chips on top of the mug brownie.
6. Enjoy the chocolate protein mug brownie warm.

Nutritional values (per serving):

- Calories: 250
- Protein: 30g
- Fat: 10g
- Carbohydrates: 10g
- Fiber: 4g

Vanilla Protein Cheesecake

Ingredients:

- 1 cup of cottage cheese
- 1 scoop of vanilla protein powder
- 2 tablespoons of almond flour
- 2 tablespoons of Greek yogurt
- 2 tablespoons of honey
- 1/2 teaspoon of vanilla extract
- Optional: Fresh berries for topping

Directions:

1. In a blender or food processor, combine the cottage cheese, vanilla protein powder, almond flour, Greek yogurt, honey, and vanilla extract. Blend until smooth and creamy.
2. Pour the mixture into individual serving dishes or a single pie dish.
3. Refrigerate the cheesecake for at least 2 hours to set.
4. Serve the vanilla protein cheesecake chilled, topped with fresh berries if desired.

Nutritional values (per serving):

- Calories: 200
- Protein: 30g
- Fat: 5g
- Carbohydrates: 10g
- Fiber: 1g

Peanut Butter Protein Cookies

Ingredients:

- 1 cup of almond flour
- 1/2 cup of vanilla protein powder
- 1/4 cup of peanut butter
- 1/4 cup of honey
- 1 egg
- 1/2 teaspoon of vanilla extract
- Optional: Dark chocolate chips for topping

Directions:

1. Preheat the oven to 350°F (180°C). Line a baking sheet with parchment paper.
2. In a bowl, mix together the almond flour, vanilla protein powder, peanut butter, honey, egg, and vanilla extract until a dough forms.
3. Roll the dough into small balls and place them on the prepared baking sheet. Flatten each ball slightly with a fork.
4. Optional: Press a few dark chocolate chips onto the top of each cookie.
5. Bake the cookies in the preheated oven for about 12-15 minutes, or until golden brown.
6. Let the cookies cool on the baking sheet before transferring to a wire rack to cool completely.

Nutritional values (per cookie):

- Calories: 100
- Protein: 8g
- Fat: 6g
- Carbohydrates: 6g
- Fiber: 1g

Chocolate Protein Chia Pudding

Ingredients:

- 2 tablespoons of chia seeds
- 1 scoop of chocolate protein powder
- 1 cup of unsweetened almond milk
- 1 tablespoon of unsweetened cocoa powder
- 1 tablespoon of honey or your preferred sweetener
- Optional toppings: Fresh berries, sliced almonds

Directions:

1. In a bowl, whisk together the chia seeds, chocolate protein powder, unsweetened almond milk, cocoa powder, and honey.
2. Let the mixture sit for about 5 minutes, then whisk again to break up any clumps.
3. Cover the bowl and refrigerate for at least 2 hours or overnight, allowing the chia seeds to absorb the liquid and form a pudding-like consistency.
4. Stir the chia pudding before serving.
5. Top with fresh berries and sliced almonds, if desired.
6. Enjoy the chocolate protein chia pudding chilled.

Nutritional values (per serving):

- Calories: 200
- Protein: 20g
- Fat: 8g
- Carbohydrates: 15g
- Fiber: 8g

Vanilla Protein Ice Cream

Ingredients:

- 2 cups of Greek yogurt
- 1 scoop of vanilla protein powder
- 1 tablespoon of honey or your preferred sweetener
- 1 teaspoon of vanilla extract
- Optional toppings: Chopped nuts, fresh fruit

Directions:

1. In a bowl, combine the Greek yogurt, vanilla protein powder, honey, and vanilla extract. Stir until well combined.
2. Pour the mixture into an ice cream maker and churn according to the manufacturer's instructions until it reaches a soft-serve consistency.
3. Transfer the ice cream to a lidded container and freeze for at least 2 hours to firm up.
4. Scoop the vanilla protein ice cream into bowls or cones.
5. Top with chopped nuts and fresh fruit, if desired.
6. Enjoy the vanilla protein ice cream frozen.

Nutritional values (per serving):

- Calories: 150
- Protein: 20g
- Fat: 2g
- Carbohydrates: 12g
- Fiber: 0g

Protein Brownie Bites

Ingredients:

- 1 cup of almond flour
- 1/4 cup of chocolate protein powder
- 1/4 cup of unsweetened cocoa powder
- 1/4 cup of honey or your preferred sweetener
- 1/4 cup of almond butter
- 1/4 cup of unsweetened almond milk
- 1 teaspoon of vanilla extract
- Optional toppings: Dark chocolate chips, chopped nuts

Directions:

1. In a bowl, mix together the almond flour, chocolate protein powder, unsweetened cocoa powder, honey, almond butter, almond milk, and vanilla extract until well combined.
2. Roll the mixture into small bite-sized balls and place them on a baking sheet lined with parchment paper.
3. Optional: Press a few dark chocolate chips or chopped nuts onto the top of each brownie bite.
4. Refrigerate the brownie bites for at least 1 hour to firm up.
5. Store the protein brownie bites in an airtight container in the refrigerator for up to one week.
6. Enjoy the protein brownie bites chilled.

Nutritional values (per serving, based on 1 bite):

- Calories: 80
- Protein: 5g
- Fat: 5g
- Carbohydrates: 6g
- Fiber: 1g

Peanut Butter Protein Shake

Ingredients:

- 1 scoop of chocolate or vanilla protein powder
- 1 cup of unsweetened almond milk
- 1 tablespoon of peanut butter
- 1/2 banana
- Ice cubes (optional)

Directions:

1. In a blender, combine the protein powder, almond milk, peanut butter, and banana.
2. Blend until smooth and creamy.
3. If desired, add ice cubes and blend again for a thicker consistency.
4. Pour the peanut butter protein shake into a glass and enjoy.

Nutritional values (per serving):

- Calories: 250
- Protein: 25g
- Fat: 10g
- Carbohydrates: 15g
- Fiber: 3g

Protein Pancakes with Berries

Ingredients:

- 1 scoop of vanilla protein powder
- 1/4 cup of almond flour
- 1/4 teaspoon of baking powder

- 1/4 teaspoon of cinnamon
- 2 egg whites
- 1/4 cup of unsweetened almond milk
- 1/2 teaspoon of vanilla extract
- Fresh berries for topping

Directions:

1. In a bowl, whisk together the vanilla protein powder, almond flour, baking powder, and cinnamon.
2. In a separate bowl, whisk the egg whites, almond milk, and vanilla extract until well combined.
3. Add the wet ingredients to the dry ingredients and stir until a smooth batter forms.
4. Heat a non-stick skillet or griddle over medium heat and lightly coat it with cooking spray.
5. Pour about 1/4 cup of the batter onto the skillet to form each pancake.
6. Cook the pancakes for about 2-3 minutes on each side, or until golden brown and cooked through.
7. Serve the protein pancakes topped with fresh berries.

Nutritional values (per serving):

- Calories: 200
- Protein: 25g
- Fat: 6g
- Carbohydrates: 10g
- Fiber: 2g

Chocolate Protein Mousse

Ingredients:

- 1 cup of Greek yogurt

- 1 scoop of chocolate protein powder
- 1 tablespoon of unsweetened cocoa powder
- 1 tablespoon of honey or your preferred sweetener
- 1/2 teaspoon of vanilla extract
- Optional toppings: Shredded coconut, sliced almonds

Directions:

1. In a bowl, mix together the Greek yogurt, chocolate protein powder, cocoa powder, honey, and vanilla extract until smooth and well combined.
2. Spoon the mixture into serving glasses or bowls.
3. Optional: Top with shredded coconut and sliced almonds for added texture and flavor.
4. Refrigerate the chocolate protein mousse for at least 1 hour to set.
5. Enjoy the chocolate protein mousse chilled.

Nutritional values (per serving):

- Calories: 150
- Protein: 20g
- Fat: 2g
- Carbohydrates: 10g
- Fiber: 2g

Strawberry Protein Smoothie Bowl

Ingredients:

- 1 scoop of strawberry protein powder
- 1 cup of frozen strawberries
- 1/2 banana
- 1/2 cup of unsweetened almond milk
- Toppings: Fresh berries, sliced almonds, chia seeds

Directions:

1. In a blender, combine the strawberry protein powder, frozen strawberries, banana, and almond milk.
2. Blend until smooth and creamy.
3. Pour the smoothie into a bowl.
4. Top with fresh berries, sliced almonds, and chia seeds.
5. Enjoy the strawberry protein smoothie bowl with a spoon.

Nutritional values (per serving):

- Calories: 250
- Protein: 25g
- Fat: 6g
- Carbohydrates: 25g
- Fiber: 6g

Chocolate Protein Chia Seed Pudding

Ingredients:

- 2 tablespoons of chia seeds
- 1 scoop of chocolate protein powder
- 1 cup of unsweetened almond milk
- 1 tablespoon of unsweetened cocoa powder
- 1 tablespoon of honey or your preferred sweetener
- Toppings: Sliced almonds, shredded coconut

Directions:

1. In a bowl, whisk together the chia seeds, chocolate protein powder, almond milk, cocoa powder, and honey.
2. Let the mixture sit for about 5 minutes, then whisk again to break up any clumps.

3. Cover the bowl and refrigerate for at least 2 hours or overnight, allowing the chia seeds to absorb the liquid and form a pudding-like consistency.
4. Stir the chia seed pudding before serving.
5. Top with sliced almonds and shredded coconut.
6. Enjoy the chocolate protein chia seed pudding chilled.

Nutritional values (per serving):

- Calories: 200
- Protein: 20g
- Fat: 8g
- Carbohydrates: 15g
- Fiber: 10g

Vanilla Protein Energy Balls

Ingredients:

- 1 cup of rolled oats
- 1/2 cup of vanilla protein powder
- 1/4 cup of almond butter
- 1/4 cup of honey or your preferred sweetener
- 1/4 cup of dark chocolate chips
- 1 teaspoon of vanilla extract

Directions:

1. In a bowl, mix together the rolled oats, vanilla protein powder, almond butter, honey, dark chocolate chips, and vanilla extract until well combined.
2. Roll the mixture into bite-sized balls.
3. Place the energy balls in the refrigerator for at least 30 minutes to firm up.

4. Store the vanilla protein energy balls in an airtight container in the refrigerator for up to one week.
5. Enjoy the energy balls as a quick and nutritious snack.

Nutritional values (per serving, based on 1 ball):

- Calories: 100
- Protein: 8g
- Fat: 5g
- Carbohydrates: 8g
- Fiber: 1g

Vanilla Protein Panna Cotta

Ingredients:

- 1 scoop of vanilla protein powder
- 1 cup of unsweetened almond milk
- 1 tablespoon of gelatin powder
- 1 tablespoon of honey or sweetener of choice
- 1/2 teaspoon of vanilla extract
- Optional toppings: Fresh berries, mint leaves

Directions:

1. In a small saucepan, heat the almond milk over medium heat until it starts to simmer.
2. In a separate bowl, combine the vanilla protein powder and gelatin powder.
3. Slowly pour the hot almond milk into the bowl while whisking constantly until the powders are fully dissolved.
4. Stir in the honey and vanilla extract.
5. Divide the mixture into ramekins or small bowls.
6. Refrigerate the panna cotta for at least 2 hours, or until it sets and becomes firm.

7. Before serving, top with fresh berries and mint leaves if desired.

Nutritional values (per serving):

- Calories: 150
- Protein: 15g
- Fat: 3g
- Carbohydrates: 10g
- Fiber: 0g

Chocolate Peanut Butter Protein Balls

Ingredients:

- 1 cup of rolled oats
- 1/2 cup of chocolate protein powder
- 1/2 cup of natural peanut butter
- 1/4 cup of honey or sweetener of choice
- 1/4 cup of dark chocolate chips
- 1 teaspoon of vanilla extract

Directions:

1. In a food processor, blend the rolled oats until they become a fine powder.
2. In a large mixing bowl, combine the oat powder, chocolate protein powder, peanut butter, honey, dark chocolate chips, and vanilla extract.
3. Stir well until all the ingredients are fully combined.
4. Shape the mixture into small balls using your hands.
5. Place the protein balls on a baking sheet lined with parchment paper.
6. Refrigerate the balls for at least 1 hour to firm up.

7. Store the chocolate peanut butter protein balls in an airtight container in the refrigerator.

Nutritional values (per serving, based on 1 ball):

- Calories: 100
- Protein: 6g
- Fat: 4g
- Carbohydrates: 10g
- Fiber: 2g

CONCLUSION

In conclusion, this protein-rich cookbook serves as a comprehensive guide to nourishing your body with essential nutrients without compromising on flavor. Whether you're a fitness enthusiast, a professional athlete, or simply someone interested in a protein-focused diet, the versatile recipes in this book cater to a wide array of tastes and dietary preferences.

From breakfast to dinner, with snacks and desserts in between, these protein-packed recipes are meticulously crafted to ensure you receive the necessary protein for your body's growth, repair, and optimal function. The ease and simplicity of these recipes further encourages a healthy lifestyle, providing you with meals that are not only nutritious but also appealing and enjoyable.

As you journey through this cookbook, remember that a diet rich in protein is not just for muscle gain. It's a lifestyle choice that contributes to overall health, strength, and wellbeing. Your adventure in protein-rich cooking doesn't have to stop here; continue to explore, experiment, and personalize these recipes as per your unique preferences.

We hope that this cookbook proves to be more than just a recipe guide for you, but rather a source of inspiration, leading you towards a healthier and more balanced lifestyle. Enjoy the process of discovering and creating these protein-rich meals, and most importantly, savor and appreciate the delicious, nutritious food you've prepared. After all, the journey to health and wellness is always the most rewarding when it's enjoyed.